THERE'S ALWAYS ANOTHER HILL!

How NOT to cycle from
John o' Groats to Land's End

FRED JOHNSON

DB PUBLISHING

This book is dedicated to the memory of Gwen and to Chris who gave me the most important thing in the world, their love.

Also to the memory of Tom Simson.
The heroes of one's youth remain giants forever.

I would also like to thank Bill and John, without whom the ride would never have happened.

First published in Great Britain in 2012 by The Derby Books Publishing Company Limited, 3 The Parker Centre, Derby, DE21 4SZ.

ISBN 978-1-78091-050-5
Printed and bound by CPI Antony Rowe, Chippenham.

CONTENTS

Chapter 1

YOU CAN TIE A KNOT WITH YOUR TONGUE THAT YOU CAN'T UNDO WITH YOUR TEETH

It all started innocently enough, as most of life's major catastrophes usually do. I was casually talking to a work colleague one lunchtime, when I inadvertently set in motion a cycle (no pun intended) of events that were going to lead me over the next nine months to heartache, agony and pain. Let this be a lesson to all sane, rational, right thinking people, sometimes the most innocent of comments can lead you into situations that you could only experience in your worst nightmares. Don't sneer and think you're superior and it couldn't happen to you, because believe me it could.

You may ask, what in an ordinary conversation with a friend at work could result in such dramatic earth shattering consequences? Well I will tell you, I had simply asked this guy what he had planned for that night after work. If I'd known what those few simple words were going to cost me, I can tell you now I would never have uttered them; in fact, I would have been grateful if the good Lord had struck me dumb on the spot that very instant.

Bill was, to all intents and purposes, a down to earth, dead average guy the likes of you, me and thousands of others who you come across every day. At that time, even though I had only known him a month or two, he had never given any sort of hint or indication that he was totally insane.

He had a cheerful disposition, slightly built about the same height as me and, guessing, I would say in his mid 40s. Alright he had a bit of a chip on his shoulder regarding women, but hey, who gets to their mid 40s with nothing to complain about regarding women and though I can't pretend to be an expert in such things, I've no doubt it's the same for women regarding men. I meanwhile was 54, balding, 5ft 8in and not so much hovering as rapidly sliding down the wrong side of 14 stone.

Anyway, in answer to my question he replied 'Oh, I was thinking of going out on the bike.' Now, not in the stretch of anyone's imagination would you think this was going to be the opening gambit to a nightmare scenario. Alas, due to the twists and turns of fate and no small thanks to my big mouth it was, and the worst of it was I never even saw it coming – you may laugh but I bet you wouldn't have either.

I must admit I have been a reasonably keen bike rider myself at various times during my life, from when I was a teenager to later when I used to go out cycling with my son when he was a teenager. So I replied quite simply, 'I used to do quite a bit of cycling myself. What sort of bike do you have?' I expected him to say a mountain bike, which were all the rage about that time.

'It's a road bike' he replied.

'Oh, I've got a road bike' I chimed in, glad to meet a fellow cyclist of my own persuasion. 'I love riding on the road, I find it so exhilarating. The feeling of freedom and the ability to travel long distances quickly, efficiently and cheaply, I think there's nothing like it. I never fancied mountain biking, I never much liked going up hills, in fact, with my build my speciality if I had one, would have been downhill cycling.'

So in all innocence I carried on and getting a bit carried away with the thought of cycling again I said, 'Look Bill, I could do with losing some weight and getting fit, if I get on my bike again, in a few weeks once I get myself into the swing of things, perhaps we could go out for a ride together one weekend.' Bill seemed delighted to have found a possible companion for his rides.

'Yes I would love to' he said, 'It would be good to have some company.'

The conversation went on harmlessly about bikes and cycling in general for about 10 minutes, all pleasant enough stuff. Then all at once, although I didn't realise it at the time, the very first inklings of Bill's madness began to creep to the surface.

'Do you know Fred?' He said in a quite relaxed tone of voice, 'I'll tell you what I've always fancied,' now this was delivered as calm as you like, his features never changed, I would never in a million years have dreamed of what was coming next. So I walked straight into it and I still maintain to this day anyone else would have done the same. God I could cry even now when I think back on my unbelievably inane stupidity.

'What'? I asked.

'Cycling from John o' Groats to Land's End' he says.

Now this was when the alarm bells should have rung loud and clear, I should have smelt the danger, seen what was coming, made my excuses and got back to work quicker than you could say Lance Armstrong. But as always, at times like this there's that little devil that sits on your shoulders and takes the most perverse pleasure in dropping you in it from a great height. Therefore, instead of tactfully changing the subject as I should have, I sat there and innocently took the bait, hook, line and sinker.

'Oh, I've done that once.' I said. As soon as the words were out of my mouth I started to feel a bit uneasy, but then again as a lot of my friends will tell you I was never the sharpest chisel in the box.

Bill's eyes lit up, 'Have you?'

'Yes,' I answered 'about three years ago, to raise money for cancer research after my wife died of malignant melanoma.'

Bill's face was a picture, 'What was it like?' He asked.

Now, this was the critical moment, had I played my cards right there was still, albeit a slim, possibility that I had a chance to recover the situation at this point, but no. When that devil's riding your back, you've got the blinkers on and he's got his spurs stuck in to your backside, you're only going one way pal.

So like the total fool I was, I recounted some of the details to him. Now I don't know if you have experienced this, but the mind is a wonderful thing. When you look back on something from so long ago you tend to forget the bad things. Your mind can't recollect the actual feeling of the pain, it only remembers the good times. A psychologist would probably say it's something to do with the body's recovery system or self preservation. Yes, well in this case it near as damn finished me off, so much for psychologists!

Anyway, so it was with me, like the stupid fool I was I told him about the good days, the sun on your back, the wind behind you, bowling along at a nice speed, the comradeship, a good hot shower at night followed by a nice meal in the pub and a couple of pints.

'It sounds like you had a good time.' Bill says to me beaming. Of course, being the stupid pratt that I am, I didn't realise I was committing suicide, so I couldn't leave it at that, oh no I had to go into greater details, of the exhilaration of finishing at Land's End, cracking open a bottle of Champagne or two and then getting a skinful in the bar while we were waiting for our arrival photographs to be developed, then out to the pub again that evening celebrating.

When I look back now, from all these years away, I cannot think of a crasser, more mind-numbing, cretinous act of sheer stupidity since the Charge of the Light Brigade. I may as well have taken a gun, pointed it at my head and blown my brains out. By the time I had finished, Bill was looking like it was his birthday, Christmas and every other great event in his life rolled into one. He was literally bouncing from one foot to the other as if he was going to burst with excitement.

'Fabulous! It sounds great; will you do it with me?' The mad fool, he blurted it out like he was just asking me to pop out to the corner shop with him.

Too late, I realised the enormity of my error and suddenly my mind brought back the rest of it. All the hours, days and weeks of training in all weathers, fitting it in after work and at weekends. Month after month of going out on your bike, when it was dark, when it was cold and when it was miserable. Then the actual trip, the 100 miles a day, the rain, battling against the driving wind, flogging your body up mountains with every muscle screaming to stop but knowing if you did you would never get started again. Then last but not least, the traffic, always at your back hearing the pneumatics as the wagons were breaking, changing gear or revving the engine as they try to get past on narrow lanes. Or flying past you within 3ft at 60, 70 and 80 miles per hour and I can tell you sometimes you could feel the suction trying to pull you in to them.

Oh yes, it all came flooding back alright and there was this idiot guy in front of me smiling from ear to ear like someone not right. All at once the picture was crystal clear, I suddenly decided that something had to be done to get me out of this horrendous situation I found myself in. So I started to blurt out all these other things, the things I should have said at first instead of painting the rosy picture I had, what a waste of time, he wasn't listening.

'Come on Fred, you said you wanted to get fit and lose weight and you've done it once, you would know what to expect.'

I was beginning to panic by this time, 'Yes I bl**dy do know what to expect and I can tell you now I've no intention of doing it again,' I choked, but his face was alight. He wasn't right, he was in hyper-drive and I could see he was set on looking for sorrow and pain and if he was going to cycle into the jaws of hell, by God he was bl**dy determined that I was going to be with him.

Thankfully lunch ended just then and it was time to get back to work. I shot back to my seat and got stuck into my work, anything to get me away from this madman. However, every time he walked past me that afternoon he had a go at me. The man was manic, he was like a Jack Russell with a rat, he just wouldn't let go. I was never so glad to see 5 o'clock in all my life. I was never one for watching the clock, but that night 5pm and my computer was off, the desk tidied and I was through that door like a bat out of hell, they didn't see me for dust.

I drove home feeling like a condemned man; how I got through the traffic I'll never know. I was determined I didn't want to do it again, but I knew Bill was not going to take no for an answer. He was going to make life uncomfortable for me for the next few days, but I was unwavering in my determination he would not succeed. It was one of those occasions when you pull up on your drive and think, God I'm here already and you can't actually remember how you got there.

I went through the front door into the house and straight upstairs, took my suit off, got changed, put my slippers on and went downstairs.

'How are you love, had a good day?' Chris asked as I went in the kitchen where she was preparing dinner.

'Err, so, so' I replied as I walked over to give her a kiss. By this time Chris could read me like a book, she looked at me wryly.

'Anything wrong love?' she asked.

'No, no nothing at all' I said trying my best to pull myself together and look normal.

'You look a bit apprehensive, as if you've something on your mind.' She said.

'Oh no, it's nothing really, just a problem we're dealing with at work, nothing to worry about.' I replied.

We had dinner and afterwards I settled down with a gin and tonic watching the television. I wasn't looking forward to going to work the next day, I had a feeling Bill was going to be a right pain.

I wasn't wrong, every time he saw me the next few days it was all he talked about, he tried all ways, telling me how great I had said it was, how it would be wonderful for my fitness. How we could raise thousands of pounds for cancer research, he really knew how to get to me.

As the days rapidly grew into a week then two, the constant badgering and him reminding me of in my words 'the great times I'd had when I did it,' I started to weaken. Finally he got the better of me but I still held on to one last hope.

'OK' I said, 'If you can get the firm to sponsor us and give us time off to do it, with pay, I'll do it with you.' That should sort it I thought, knowing the company as I did and it was a Scottish company, I was sure they would never agree to that.

I went home that night with butterflies in my stomach, I was pretty certain my brainwave was going to get me off the hook as I was sure the firm wouldn't agree to what Bill was going to propose, but just in case I thought I had better tell Chris. As soon as I walked in she could tell there was something wrong.

'What's the matter?' she asked.

'Nothing,' I snapped, as soon as the words left her mouth. Oh God! Come on get it over with I thought, tell her now. So I looked at her and blurted out the whole sorry tale.

When I'd finished she smiled, gave me a kiss and said, 'Go get yourself a drink and watch the television while I get the dinner ready and don't worry it may never happen.'

Over the next few days Bill never mentioned the ride, which filled me with a new found confidence that everything would be fine. I even started to enjoy life again; I got back in the old routine working hard during the day and a few gin and tonics with the feet up watching the television at night. However, as you all know, it's when you start to enjoy yourself and think everything in the garden is rosy, when life comes and kicks you in the teeth!

One day after a couple of weeks, I was sitting at my desk totally engrossed in a feasibility study I was doing on a piece of land. I hadn't a care in the world, everything had gone quiet for a week or so on the John o' Groats front. Bill hadn't even mentioned it for a few days but then, just when I was least expecting it, he came rushing into the office with a look on his face like he had won the lottery. The moment I saw him heading for me and saw the smile on his face I had the most awful feeling to the pit of my stomach. I knew what was coming; he didn't have to say a word.

'Great news,' he cried 'They have agreed to sponsor us and will give us half the time off with pay if we take the other half out of our holidays.'

I sat there looking up, not particularly at him, more looking through him, or really not looking at anything, I can't explain how I felt. I just sat unable to say anything, feeling totally numb for what seemed like a lifetime. When I finally got a grip of myself and focused on his face, he was beaming with pure, unadulterated joy. With God as my witness, I could have got up and thumped him in the face until I was dragged off. Then, after the first shock had passed I realised that I didn't really want to hit him, what I really, really would have liked to do was just go somewhere quiet and cry.

So, that was the beginning of a very sorry story, my story, or more exactly, the story of how I finished up cycling from John o' Groats to Land's End for a second time when I should have known better. Now there's nothing fantastic about that you may say and I agree, but then again you may be among the millions of people who have had the good sense not to do it.

Alright, I know there are hundreds of people in this world who have done it once, twice, even a dozen times and other things a million times more difficult, I realise this. However, you would be surprised at how many nutcases there are in this world, or then again perhaps you wouldn't and most of these people are well trained, have teams behind them to sort diets and training regimes etc., not just washed up, past it types like me.

I have written this story, not for them, not for the super fit or the super heroes, or the super fools, it's for the likes of you and me, the normal straightforward everyday Joes with very nice, comfortable, boring lives thank you. People who just go about their business, in fact, the majority of the population who just quietly carry on and never want to do anything out of the ordinary or totally stupid with their lives, in other words, the intelligent ones.

Now as you don't know me from Adam, I had better give you a bit of my background, keeping it as short as possible, not wanting to bore you. If you're about my age and were brought up in a similar environment it will seem an all too familiar story anyway, but it may give you an insight into why a normally sane man should finish up doing stupid things at a time in his life when he should be relaxing.

I was born in an ordinary post-war family in a Lancashire mill town called Radcliffe in 1948. I was actually born in my grandmother's (my father's mother) house, why I can only guess but I'm not certain. It was probably something to do with my father being away a lot and my grandmother having a council house which had, of course, hot and cold water, a bath and inside toilet, luxuries that for our little family would be a long while coming. Obviously, my mother thought it would be better for her and me and there would also be someone to help out with my elder sister.

From all reports I am lucky to be here at all, as apparently on the night I was born, one of my dad's brothers who was still at home had decided to keep chickens and had got some new born chicks which he had put under the stairs with a kerosene lamp to keep them warm during the night.

The theory behind this seems to elude me now, why he couldn't leave them with the hen I don't know I can only surmise that he'd bought the chicks and didn't have a hen. Anyway, whether one of the chicks knocked the lamp over or what no one knows, but the thing spilled and a fire started under the stairs. Well from all the stories I have heard there was all round panic, apart of course, from me, and the fire brigade had to be called to get us out and put the fire out.

The family consisted of my mother, father and much older sister Marian; well she seemed much older at the time but was actually seven when I was born. We didn't have much, but most of the people who were born around us about the same time were just the same. We lived in a rented two up two down terraced house, the type that was everywhere at that time around most mill towns, cities and their environs.

The houses in the square in which we lived had all been recently renovated, there was just cold water and a coal fire but we did have electric lights and a two ring gas burner stove in the kitchen, unlike my other grandmother (my mother's mother) who only had gas lights and a fireside range. We had our own toilet, outside, one of a block of six in a communal yard shared by five other houses and it was damned cold on a winter's night I can tell you.

A galvanised metal bath hung on a nail on the outside wall at the side of the back door which every weekend was religiously taken into the house, filled by boiling the kettle and we would all have a bath whether we needed it or not! Marian would bathe first then me as I was considered dirtier than my sister, then we would go to bed after which my mother bathed, followed last by my dad, all in the same water just topped up with more warm from the kettle.

We had linoleum on the living room floor with a square of carpet in the middle, an old leatherette (whatever that was) settee, two chairs and a small dining table against the back wall. My mother was very proud of her home as most people were in those days, everything was kept spotless. They swept the footpath in front of the house and donkey stoned the front step and window sill with a stone they got off the rag and bone man who came round every month or so. I remember her telling people in later life, how in those days they could leave their front doors unlocked and no one would steal anything. I remember thinking at the time; yes, the reason was in those days we didn't have anything worth stealing, that's why.

I couldn't say times were hard, they were no harder than for all my mates, we didn't know any different. What I will say is that we always had good wholesome meals, though there were no luxuries as the country was still recovering from World War Two and up to being five some things were still rationed. One thing we certainly got was plenty of exercise, when we weren't at school we would be playing out all day not because of any burning desire to be fit just basically because there was nothing to do inside.

There was always something to do outside though; we could go 'up the fields' which we thought was a great adventure. Our parents would say don't go further than the first bench (a form opposite the secondary school leading into the country) or if they were in a relaxed mood they may even let us go as far as the second bench (about a further 100 yards). The reason we could not go past the second bench was that beyond that was 'The Canal', a place that would surely lure us to our certain death.

We would always agree not to go past the second bench and go chasing off, thinking it a great adventure, but the older ones among us would dare us younger ones to go to the canal and once there even further to the 'Black Cat Reservoir'. There we could watch the men fishing and see what they had caught, to us kids it was at the furthest reaches of the known world.

The fields alongside the route grew turnips and swedes, we would dig one up and one of the lads would cut it up with his knife and share it between us when we got hungry. Of course, we would get back home hours later, covered from head to foot in muck and mud on our shoes, walk in the house and before I could say two words I would get a clip round the ear from my mother. 'What's that for?' I'd cry indignantly.

'For going up to the res, that's what it's for.' She'd shout. I'd just open my mouth, about to say I hadn't been there when she'd shout, 'and don't tell me you haven't been there or you'll get another.' Knowing when I was onto a loser I kept my mouth shut, but I never could work out how she knew where we had been.

My father was often away during the week as he was a lorry driver and in those days before motorways, London to Glasgow or Edinburgh would take two days, while my mother worked at a loom in a weaving shed to supplement the family income. Though we had few treats my mother always saved enough to give us a week's holiday every year. At first it was in a caravan at Ocean Edge Caravan Park just outside Heysham, near Morecambe.

How we looked forward to our holidays, along with Christmas and Whit Friday it was the high spot of the year. We would walk up to Mills and Seddon's, the local charabanc operator with our cases and load them into the luggage areas, then pile on the coach. Marian and I would fight like cat and dog for the window seat until mother sorted us out by giving me a clip round the ear and telling Marian to swap seats halfway there. Then we would argue as to whom would sit next to the window first, as I always wanted to sit there as we were arriving to be the first to see the sea.

The caravans at Ocean Edge were the height of luxury, glass single-glazed windows which would have condensation running down them each morning, gas lights, no running water just an urn that my sister and I had to take to the site tap to fill once or twice a day and if you wanted to go to the toilet, day or night it may be a couple of minutes walk to the toilet block.

As long as I live though I will always remember the smell that the caravans had. It was a mixture of the caravan, the salty sea air and the petroleum refinery just over the headland about half a mile away. It seemed just perfect and when I look back it always reminds me of good times, childhood days, days of innocence that once left behind can never be recovered.

One of the high spots of the holiday was to walk along the coast from the campsite to Heysham docks which we did every year. I remember along the coast there were areas of large rocks where I used to jump or scramble from one to the other dodging the waves as we went along. When we arrived at Heysham docks we walked along to see what ships were in dock, this was my father's favourite bit of the holiday as he liked to expound his deep knowledge of the sea and ships to us kids. As we walked along he would get great pleasure in telling us about when he was a young man, working off the fishing boats in Great Yarmouth. My mother, however, would take great delight in deflating his ego by telling us he was actually the cook and that he used to get seasick.

After going round the docks we went on to the railway station, this was the true destination of our walk, mum and dad went into the bar and got themselves drinks, Marian and I sat outside on a form on the platform and waited for dad to come out and provide us with a soft drink and a packet of crisps. This was a special treat for us, as it was very rare you got such luxuries as bottles of pop and crisps even when we were on holiday.

By the time I was about eight we must have been getting a bit more prosperous because for our holidays it was decided we would go to Great Yarmouth in a boarding house, bed breakfast and evening meal. To me this was going to be a great adventure after the caravan at Ocean Edge. Suddenly I imagined myself getting into the real world like Philip, Jack, Dinah and Lucy Ann in Enid Blyton's 'Adventure' books which at that time I read avidly.

Suddenly I was enjoying the high life, from hunting crabs in rock pools I had switched to riding Formula 1 cars round the promenade at Yarmouth, well pedal cars anyway. Also if I say so myself I was pretty good at it, I can't remember whether we had so many laps or a set period of time but the guy who ran them would get us all lined up, then drop his flag and we would be away pedalling like mad.

I would start steadily and the others would shoot off and get well in front of me but as the race progressed I would gradually overtake them one by one and by the end I was more often than not in the lead and I would have lapped some. Little did I know that pedalling was going to be one of the things that I came to enjoy and carry on throughout my life.

I came to love Great Yarmouth and Norfolk, especially the Broads. In fact, later on in my life, after I had got married, my wife and our two children went to live in a village called Potter Heigham where we stayed for four very happy years. From this time on, however, we went nowhere else but Great Yarmouth, in fact, not until I was 18 and I went with a mate to what at that time was all the rage, a Butlin's holiday camp at Pwllheli did I go anywhere else. I could recount some wild happenings there but the millions of my generation who had holidays at Butlins would know exactly what I mean.

I spent all my life outside of school with a gang of close mates, winter or summer we lived outside if the weather was fine. The gang had a hard core of about six boys, there was I suppose what people would now call a certain amount of bullying but nothing vicious like it would appear it can be today. It would be what you could call sorting out the pecking order and once that was established everything went smoothly. That is, until someone rebelled and decided to increase their standing then there may be another sorting out session.

Although I was rooted very much at the bottom of the pecking order at the time, it never occurred to me that all the other boys apart from one, were between six and 18 months older than me, which when you are five or six makes a bit of difference. It did though eventually teach me how to stand up for and look after myself.

As a child, in fact, throughout my life, I was never fast at any sport like running and swimming. However, what I did have was a reasonable level of stamina, grim determination and pig-headed stubbornness. This was probably developed from the years of being at the bottom of the pecking order and bred in me a belief that if I couldn't beat them for speed I would bl**dy well bore them to death and keep going as long as it took.

The earliest manifestations of this determination and doggedness first came out when as children we would run around what we called 'The Square', this was the street in which we lived, which was called Waverley Place. There was one main entrance that came off School Street, it passed between a house and a row of shops and offices. It was a cobbled street approximately 20 yards long alongside the gable of an office and the gable and yard wall of the house on School Street. In front of you was the gable end of one of the rows of houses in Waverley Place. As you got to the end of the yard wall you turned left and the square opened up before you. It was bounded on the south by the rear yard walls of the houses on School Street, on the west, north and east by rows of houses facing inwards forming the square.

At the top there was an entrance onto the Recreation Ground where we used to play. It was a large area of ground about the size of a football pitch with a slide, swings, rocking horse and a couple of see-saws.

Around the perimeter was a trimmed hawthorn hedge about four feet high at that time.

The houses had no front gardens so all around the square was the standard six foot wide flagged footpath, butting up to the flags was a three foot wide strip of cobbles and all the centre of the square was tarmac (a very recent surface for the likes of our street, in fact, a lot of the main roads in the area were still cobbled at that time).

This cobbled track around the square was our race track; we would have different lengths of race: one lap, two laps or 20 laps, whatever was agreed. I would always trail in last on the shorter races but on the occasions when we did multiple laps I would always gain on the others or they would get fed up and stop before finishing. I however, always kept on; even if everyone else had dropped out I would run on my own and finish the requisite number of laps.

My greatest victory, as I remember, had a relevance to my later exploits though I would never have guessed what I would finish up doing at that time. We were on the 'Rec' on our bikes, when I say bikes I think there was only one lad who had what was a half decent bike, the rest of us had old bangers put together from all sorts of bits. In fact, it was not until my 13th birthday that I became the proud owner of a new bike.

It was decided we would have a 100 laps of the 'Rec' race. By the end of lap 30 there were a couple of us left cycling round, by the end of lap 40 I was on my own, everyone else had got fed up and disappeared. You would think that would be enough, I had got the moral victory and no one would know anyway if I finished then. But no, young Fred had to carry on and do the full 100 laps. I thought this showed my great determination and single mindedness, what the independent observer may have made of it I'll leave it up to you to decide.

By the time I was 12, I had gone to secondary school, my sister Marian had got married and moved out and we had moved house about a mile away from 'the Square' to a house in Irwell Street on the other side of town. This time my parents were purchasing it instead of renting as before. Again, it was basically a two up two down with no bathroom and an outside toilet but this time there had been a toilet installed inside as well. What luxury, never having to go outside in the dark and freezing cold in the middle of winter just to go to the toilet.

For a 12-year-old the house was brilliantly situated, it backed onto a large extremely hilly park with plenty of bushes and mature trees to climb. It had a play area with the usual swings, see-saws and an old fashioned witch's hat roundabout just behind our house. Alongside the playground there was a large shelter and a small walled off reservoir behind which we would climb into to play, at the top of the park there was also a bowling green.

At the front was a large derelict mill that had been partly on fire at one time. Also, if you went down the alleyway between the derelict mill and one that was still operating next to it, you came to Milltown Street. Turn right and in 200 yards you arrived at the 'Sailor Brow's, a large area of land on the banks of the River Irwell which fell quite steeply a couple of hundred feet from the main road at the top down to the river.

Because of all the wonderful things round about to play in, all my mates who I had grown up and went to school with when we lived in Waverley Place used to come down every night, weekends and all the school holidays. We would spend countless hours on the park or the Sailor Brow's and we explored the derelict factory till we got to know every inch of the place. We used to go in at night and a few times someone must have informed the police, because several times we were chased but we would always escape running up and down the four floors and through passages to shake them off.

The gang, as we became known, finished up consisting of about 14, quite evenly split between boys and girls and we stuck together basically until we finished school. I left school in April 1963, I was just 15, as it happened Easter was quite late that year and my birthday was on 12 April so I could leave earlier than had Easter been in March.

I got a job as an apprentice joiner at a time when if the tradesman said jump you asked 'how high?' Unlike today, if the tradesman threatened to give you a bl**dy good hiding he could and get away with it. A lot of things have changed now, some say for the better and they may well be right, I will leave that up to history to decide.

As I mentioned earlier, I was 13 when I got my new bicycle and first became interested in cycling. A friend and I used to go out at night 'training' and at weekends we would take some money and a packed lunch and shoot off to the Trough of Bowland or round Cheshire for the day. We both got quite keen for a while, even going so far as giving up smoking to improve our performance, but nothing ever came of it, apart from a deep and long lasting enjoyment of getting out on a bike and the feeling of freedom and fitness that it gives you.

Chapter 2

IT'S A LONG, LONG, HARD JOURNEY TO THE START

Well I suppose it's time to get back to the subject, so the die had been well and truly cast, I was committed to cycle from John o' Groats to Land's End again. I drove home that night from work in a trance, as I arrived home I walked into the house and the first thing I did was go into the dining room, over to the drinks cabinet and pour myself a really large gin and tonic. I walked into the kitchen and opened the fridge to get the ice; Chris was there preparing dinner, she looked at me surprised.

'Starting early tonight darling?' She said, as I dropped the two pieces of ice into the glass. I didn't answer, she looked at my face and said, 'What's the matter you look like you've lost a tenner and found a penny?'

That was it! That was the catalyst to let me get everything off my chest. 'The world's the matter' I replied. 'Gordon Bennett' I cried, 'Is there nothing sacred in this world anymore? Can you not rely on anything? At one time you could rely on your company to be miserable gits, especially Scottish companies who wouldn't part with a brass farthing if they didn't have to. But it would appear that these days they are all falling over themselves to be good members of the community and out-do each other in their damn cynical benevolence.'

Chris waited patiently while I finished my tirade then quietly asked, 'What is the matter?'

'What's the matter? What's the matter! I'll tell you what the bl**dy matter is, I'm committed to cycle from John o' Groats to Land's End again with that lunatic Bill.' I cried. 'The bl**dy firm has agreed to pay us for half the time and give a good donation to our charity.'

'Well that seems quite good' she says.

'Quite good! Quite good! I didn't bl**dy want them to give us the time off. Do you not see? Now they have agreed to all this I can't back out without looking a right pratt. He's got me in a corner and there's only one way out and it's a bl**dy long hard one, which will end up with my body being battered, going through a week of hell and all I will have to show for it will be a sore arse.'

'Never mind love,' she said 'It will do you good and you may lose some weight.'

'Lose some weight!' I looked at her as if she was mad, 'I can think of easier ways of losing weight, bl**dy hell you're beginning to sound like Bill.' I sat down with my drink, after a few moments Chris came over and gave me a kiss.

'Come on love I know you can do it' she said softly, 'and you'll do it better than last time.' I sat there and looked at my glass, the ice was melting quickly. I was calming down a bit as I looked up at her.

'Thanks love, do you know, I don't know what I would do without you.'

'Don't be daft, anyway thanks for what?' she asked laughing.

'For being you,' I replied, 'and always supporting me whatever lunatic things I dream up or get involved in.' She smiled down at me.

'Darling, I will always be here for you, lunatic things or not, you can count on that and while you're away at least I will be able to get a bit of peace and quiet.'

'Cheeky sod!' I replied.

As I sat there contemplating the trip, I remembered what Bill had said, I had the advantage of doing it once before. So I thought to myself, Fred you suffered last time, this time you're going to make the most of that advantage, if you're going to do it, you're going to be prepared thoroughly for it.

The last time I had cycled from John o' Groats to Land's End three years earlier, it was 12 months after my first wife Gwen had died, I had been 51 and I made the mistake of doing it with two younger guys. One was about 28 and, as my father used to say, as fit as a butcher's dog. The other was mid to late 30s but was a road runner who had won the tour of Tameside twice and came second once, which from my running days I seemed to recollect was six races run in a week over various distances and types of terrain around Tameside. He was then running marathons in approx 2 hours 40, which, by anybody's reckoning, is no slouch.

So there I was, living alone, working near Stockport, travelling from Radcliffe where we had moved back to before Gwen died. Getting home anytime between six and seven, hitting the whisky every night, the one good thing was I enjoyed cooking. I ate pretty well, possibly too well but at least it was all good stuff not just junk food.

I did make an attempt to train rigorously but when you leave for work at 7.30 each morning and get home between six and seven at night, then have to start making your meal, doing your washing, ironing and keep the house tidy, sometimes you find it hard to keep forcing yourself out on the bike.

It wasn't until I asked round work if anyone would be good enough to let me cycle to their house in the mornings then have a shower and get changed. Then leave again at night to cycle home that I actually got into doing any sort of regular mileage during the week, it being 17 miles each way to and from work. As it happened, this kindness by the lady concerned (Chris) finished up with me much later marrying her and she has been my strength and soulmate this past 10 years and I don't know where I would be now without her.

But now, four years later having recently married Chris, I would have more time to dedicate to my training and preparation, so I looked up at her and said, 'You're right love, I can do it and this time I will be better prepared', and do you know for a minute I started to quite enjoy my gin and tonic.

So that night I started my preparations, the first thing I did was sit down at the computer and key in 'cycling John o' Groats to Land's End'. The search engine came up with several choices as you would expect but I found one which had tips from several 'end to enders' as the people who have done John o' Groats to Land's End are called, some of which I found quite useful. Two in particular were, get yourself a good training manual and buy some waterproof socks. I thought back to four years earlier when I had first done it, one morning in particular when it was pouring down when we got up and still raining when we set off at seven. I started that day with plastic bags taped round my feet with a hole cut out at the bottom for my cleats to go through. By a miracle they just about held together until the rain stopped. So that was one of the first things I ordered off the internet, two pairs of waterproof socks, I also ordered a pair of overshoes which I didn't have for the first attempt.

The third thing I ordered was a book called *The Complete Book of Long Distance Cycling: Build the Strength, Skills and Confidence to Ride as Far as you Want.* This was full of fantastic advice from equipment, planning, training regimes, diet and anything else you could think of. I used it as my cycling bible and it was invaluable. If I had taken half of all the advice it gave I would have completed the ride a lot easier than I did.

However, another of the things I benefitted from was its advice to get a heart monitor, so this was the next thing I ordered. I copied training programmes and diets; unfortunately I stuck to the diets just about as much as I stuck to the training programmes. So although my fitness improved to a certain degree, unfortunately my weight didn't come off as I would have liked.

In the meantime, Bill and I arranged to meet up and decide the logistics of the trip, the first thing we had to decide on was the third member of the team. You may think it odd looking for someone else, why not do it just the two of us. This is fine if you're going to do it self supported, but there was no way I was going to ride all that way carting all our own gear.

I had told Bill that if I was doing it with him I wanted a challenge; his challenge was the actual doing it, mine I had decided was to do it a day faster than I had the last time. So as I had done it in nine days the last time this time we had a target of eight, so we would be travelling fair distances each day. To carry our spare equipment and to save money on accommodation we would take my caravan which is a two berth, plus a tent for Bill hence the need for a third member of our team to drive the caravan and be the back up.

Having taken our caravan the last time I had done it, I knew just the guy, John had been the support driver for us on the second half of the trip from Preston to Land's End. Now support driver is a vital position and he can make the difference between the experience being easier or a damn sight harder. John was a natural, he had been caravanning over 20 years, he was meticulous, a good organizer and had loads of patience and a great sense of humour.

After Gwen had died I had been with John on many football trips abroad to Champions League games, we had shared so many good times and quite a few hairy ones as well over the years. We could recount some stories that you would have put down to silly youthfulness, not supposedly intelligent 50-year-olds, but then that's another story.

It was October when we got together and contacted John, he was thrilled with the idea of doing it again. We had hoped to do the ride the end of June beginning of July; unfortunately it would have to be towards the end of July as John would be in Spain for a month or so at the beginning of June.

I was so delighted to have him on board, it didn't matter that we couldn't do it our preferred week. So it was decided the last week in July the following year shouldn't be too bad, the light would still be good early morning to quite late and we would be unlucky knowing our weather if it was too hot. Another benefit would be that it gave us longer to prepare.

As I still had the spare wheels, tyres, inner tubes and equipment that we had got for the first ride we didn't need to organise any spare equipment. So it was now just a matter of getting down to training.

This, of course, for mere mortals is easier said than done. I must admit, while I do genuinely love cycling I'm really a fine weather cyclist at heart. When the weather's bad or if it's dark and cold in the winter you won't often find me arguing with Chris about going out training instead of staying in having a lazy evening watching television and a few gin and tonics. So I didn't start my training until the New Year when I thought the weather would be better, but who can ever account for the British weather?

A day arrived in late January, it was a nice sunny Sunday with blue skies, not too cold and no wind, the type of beautiful fresh day you sometimes get in the winter. I went out in the garden just before we went to church, it felt quite warm in the shelter of the garden and I thought what a lovely morning, today is the day to get back on the bike.

We got back from church and I stood out in the back looking down the garden to the shed at the bottom where my bike had been for the best part of four years. For a second or two I hesitated but my mind was made up; I went to the bottom of the garden and got my bike out of the shed, as I lifted it up I marvelled as I always did at how light it was.

As I said, as a child I never had a decent bike until I got my brand new Viking all steel bicycle for my birthday, but I must say it weighed a ton compared to the one I had now. This was a Trek, an American make, all aluminium and it felt wonderful compared to what I had been used to, it never failed to amaze me with how light and responsive it was. I always thought that to be on top of a really good, expensive bike must be a fantastic experience, it must respond to your slightest touch, you make it go faster with little effort then slow it down again with gentle touches on the brakes, or going downhill go through the gears, really let it go and feel the exhilaration as it flies as free as a bird.

Mine wasn't a really expensive bike, but from the first time I got on it when my son brought it home from where he worked and asked me if

I would be interested in buying it, right up to today, when I get on that bike it feels good, like it's part of me.

I walked back up to the house pushing it, looking at the flat tyres and I suddenly thought good grief! This will be the first time you've ridden this bike since you got off it when you returned from the last John o' Groats to Land's End. I stripped it down, cleaned it, reassembled and lubricated it, pumped the tyres up and it was ready to go.

I went upstairs and sorted out my cycling gear, not a simple exercise in itself as it involved climbing into the loft and finding the suitcase that it had been consigned to years previously. I selected what I thought was the best and got changed. I looked in the mirror and to say I wasn't impressed was an understatement.

Though it felt warm in the sunshine it was January therefore it wouldn't be too warm in the shadow or in the breeze, so I had put my long black cycling tights on over my shorts and standing there in front of the full length mirror I had to say I was the spitting image of Max Wall. Oh well, I thought, if you go fast enough no one will see you and if they do just hope they don't recognise you. Then if they do and all else fails just lie through your teeth and deny it was you.

As I got to the bottom of the stairs Chris was just coming out of the kitchen, 'Don't say a word.' I said as I walked towards her to go in the kitchen.

'I wouldn't dream of it.' She said, covering her mouth with her hand. 'If you have an accident don't get them to send for me will you?' Then, laughing, she disappeared into the living room.

I filled a water bottle and slipped it in the cage on the bike, got my spare inner tube and puncture outfit and stuffed them in my back pocket compartments along with a note which read in case of accident, Name Fred Johnson, phone, followed by our phone number. I was ready to go and I can tell you I was beginning to feel a bit nervous.

Chris, having recovered her composure had come to open the door for me, 'Be careful'. She said as she waved me off.

'I will.' I called back as I walked to the end of the drive, mounted the bike and waited for the road to clear, when there was a space I set my heart monitor going, reset the cycle computer and rolled off. I set off gently at first as it had been three and a half years since I had been on the bike but before long I felt like I had never been off it. I cruised down the A6 towards Stockport, not the best road in the world to go down on a push bike. You spend more time dodging potholes and stopping and starting at traffic lights than anything else. In fact, it's not the best road to go down on anything, but for my planned easy 10 mile route it was the only way.

After the first half mile which was very slightly uphill it was downhill all the way into Stockport, three miles away. I took a left about half a mile from the centre; this took me through Edgeley and past Stockport County's football ground. Unfortunately, due to the traffic and the traffic lights, it had taken me the best part of 15 minutes to do the first three miles and that had been mainly downhill.

After Edgeley I gathered some speed downhill to a roundabout at a large supermarket where I went left again towards Cheadle Hulme. I went under an old railway bridge and then the road started to climb and I began to struggle. It's nothing really, just a slope that I go up these days as if it wasn't there, but this first ride it had me gasping and in bottom gear. It was hopeless; for goodness sake, I was almost passed by a woman pushing a pram. As I slowly got my breath back, I continued along through three sets of lights, praying at each set that they would be on stop to give me a break. Sod's Law none of them were, so going along now every depression in the road seemed like a hill to climb out of and left me gasping for breath.

At the next set of lights I went left again through the centre of Cheadle Hulme. This took me down a short steep slope under the railway bridge and up the other side. The slope up the other side was only about 50m long and not the steepest slope in the world but before I was at the top I was in bottom gear looking for some lower ones and my lungs felt they were tearing apart. I can tell you now for those who haven't cycled there is nothing as disheartening as struggling up a hill and going for a lower gear only to find you haven't got one.

Good grief I thought, I'm knackered and I still have one more climb, only this one was a lot longer, though not as steep as the one I had just struggled up. I thought I had better take it easy and conserve my energy or I would never get up it. So I cycled steadily in an easy gear for the next mile or so until I swung right around a large roundabout and hit the bottom of the final climb.

I got into next to bottom gear straight away and tried to get a nice rhythm going. The hill is about 500 metres at a maximum gradient of five or six per cent with an average of three; the lungs were stretching like they hadn't for years. I had dropped into the bottom gear long before I got near the top, my legs were trembling and the sweat was running off me and dripping onto my handlebars. Sheer will-power kept me going, I kept thinking this is the last hill and then it is downhill all the way home. I swung round the next roundabout struggled up the last 50 yards and finally reached the top of the hill.

I felt like I had cycled up L'Alpe-d'Huez, my breath was coming in sobs, there was nothing left in my legs and I was struggling to focus with the sweat in my eyes but I had made it. The only trouble being, even though it was downhill now it was against the wind, so I still had to pedal with quite a bit of effort to maintain a reasonable speed. I pushed as much as I could until almost home then I dropped into a low gear and spun the rest of the way home to cool down. When I finally arrived back I stopped my heart monitor, got off the bike and staggered in.

'Goodness!' Chris exclaimed 'You look terrible, you haven't been long. How far have you been?'

As I took my helmet off and struggled with my gloves I managed to gasp '10 miles.'

'Ten Miles!' she repeated, 'You look awful; you look like you've done about 50.'

'Thanks,' I said 'You really know how to encourage someone; I'm going for a shower.' I took the bike into our outhouse lent it against the wall and fell against the other wall to get my breath back. After a few seconds I trudged upstairs, legs trembling, thinking, what in God's name have I let myself in for? The previous optimism had vanished, I stripped my cycling gear off, it was wet through with sweat, threw it in the washing basket, walked into the bathroom and ran the shower, climbed into the bath and got under the hot spray. Good Lord I thought, this is horrendous, am I ever going to do this? Then, as the hot water ran down me I started to feel a bit better and after a while I began to get that holier than thou feeling. As I started to recover I thought, yes! I've cycled 10 miles, OK it's not a lot but I did it in 45 minutes, at 55 years old and not having been on a bike for over three years that's not bad going. Let's stick with it and show Bill and everyone else I still have the determination and bottle to complete the task. I gave myself a good scrub, got dry and dressed then went into the computer room.

I took my heart monitor and cycle computer in with me, got the system up and started a spread sheet. Across the top I put the headings, Day, Date, Miles, Time, Average Heart Rate, Calories and Time in Zone. Then at the far side I had a large column for the route weather conditions and how I felt on the day. I entered the figures from my monitor and computer; they read like this, Miles-10.45, Time-44.45, Heart Rate-133, Calories-514, Time in Zone-18.08 and Miles per Hour-14.11. I stared at the figures, not being quite sure what they meant but I was pretty certain they weren't good. It still doesn't mean a lot to me but the figures for the same ride some time later read. Miles-10.45, Time-37.21, Heart Rate-121, Calories-353, Time in Zone-32.45 and Miles per Hour-16.85. These apparently showed that I had got somewhat fitter, I'm not an expert but I can tell you this, it was a sight easier getting round than it was the first time I did it.

As the weeks went by I gradually got better, it seemed a very slow process at first, the gains seemed to be negligible but in the winter and early spring the conditions aren't conducive to cycling for the likes of me. I can tell you now, cycling on a freezing February evening after work 6–7.30 in the evening is not much fun. When you get back and can't use your fingers to find the key and open the door. I used to ring the bell and Chris would open the door, take my bike off me and take my cycling helmet and gloves off, as I couldn't do it for myself. It's at times like this that you start to have doubts and begin to think you must be mad and start asking, why on earth am I doing this?

As the days turned into weeks and I was making a slow but steady improvement in my performance, we started to sort out sponsorship. We had permission from our company to approach the subcontractors and suppliers that we dealt with but not on company headed paper. So one day I rode down Chester Road in Trafford and called at the Cancer Research UK's offices. They were very obliging and provided us with a letter to confirm we were raising money on their behalf and some of their letter headed paper, posters and two T-shirts to wear.

We soon had a list of all the people and companies we were about to approach and had a letter drafted explaining what we were doing and what it was in aid of to send along with a copy of the Cancer Research letter. Alongside this, we also phoned quite a few to speak to them personally. Once the letters were in the post it was just a matter of getting on with our training and sitting back to see what offers came in.

Sometime after, Bill came across to me and said he had been talking to someone about our ride and that he had told them that we were raising money for cancer research. Apparently this person knew of a group of ladies who raised a lot of money for the same charity. They were known as the Ribble Valley Ladies Luncheon Club and if I didn't mind could we donate it into their fund? As I wasn't fussed so long as it went to cancer research I told him I had no objections so that was agreed.

After what seemed an eternity the days started to get longer and the weather a bit warmer, I began to enjoy my cycling a bit more. During the early months of the year I did a programme on the computer which was really impressive. It showed every day all the way up to the event with the target mileage for each day, with a column alongside for the actual mileage. Had I stuck to it I have no doubt the experience I was going to have would have been much better than it finished up. But, unfortunately, as the weeks progressed the gap between the projected mileages and the actual got wider and wider and it wasn't on the positive side.

I had devised a series of routes, all of them being left-handed circular so that there were as few right hand turns as possible. These routes varied from the initial 10 miles, going up to 20, 25, 30 and one about 60 which was the one Bill and I would do when he came over to ours on a Sunday.

We cycled together about once every two to three weeks, we would take it in turns, one weekend I would drive to his house at Wigan and we would do about 50 to 60 miles. Then the next time he would drive to ours and we would do the same. The trouble was we only did this about eight times over the spring and early summer.

Remembering how I suffered on the climbs the first time, I thought I would do some effective hill work. It would have been even more effective if I could have got my weight down from the 14 stone plus to the 12 and a half I had aimed for. But my weight just obstinately stuck at 13 and a half stone and I couldn't lose an ounce after that.

I realise now if I had cut out the alcohol during the week I would have made it, as just before I became 60, I went on a serious diet and managed to get from 14 stone 10 down to 12 and a half stone between 1 January and 12 April, my birthday, and that was without cycling.

Once a week I used to ride up the steepest hill near us which went from the Macclesfield Road up through Pott Shrigley and Kettleshulme then down to Whaley Bridge. This was a 24 mile round circuit and it's roughly half an hour of solid climbing, for me that is. The first time I attempted to do it I must have stopped about a dozen times.

I'll always remember one day when I was about three quarters of the way to the top, I was struggling up the hill gasping for breath doing about three miles per hour. After struggling like hell and my front wheel wobbling trying to keep going and not fall off I finally stopped gasping for breath when this cyclist passed me.

'Nice day for a ride.' He said, as he cycled passed.

He must have been 10 years older than me, but he was on a mountain bike and where my legs were trembling to push my 42 tooth chain ring and 25 tooth cog round he was pedalling away like a good one with his what I would guess was something like a 36 tooth chain ring. I thought then almost 10 years ago that I must get a better gearing on my bike for going up hills, but it is only in the last 12 months I have actually done it. However, one day I finally got up without stopping after about six or eight attempts and I can tell you I felt pretty damned pleased about it, even if I was totally exhausted when I got to the top.

As the date for our departure got closer I sent my bike in to the local bike shop for a complete service, new tyres, cables and brake blocks and while it was in I asked them to fit STI levers as it still had a frame mounted changer for the gears. I am sure you have all experienced times in your life when one moment you are saying 'oh we have plenty of time,' then before you realise it, it is nearly upon you. So it was with us, I had so much training and preparation still to do but unfortunately it was too late, the time had come to suffer.

Before we knew it the fateful weekend was upon us, six months before I was ready for it. The Thursday evening before we were due to set off, I sat there with my gin and tonic thinking of all the opportunities I had missed to get really fit for the ride. I thought about Chris and how she would have to sit at home wondering where I was and how I was doing, whether or not I would come home safe but more than that, I thought about myself, how would I cope? Would I get up the hills? Would I make it to Land's End or would it be a disaster?

The dangers didn't bother me too much even though, unfortunately, these days it's not really something I would recommend lightly. Most drivers are great and make allowances for cyclists, especially if you give clear indication of what you intend to do. But there are some I'm afraid like in any section of the community or walk of life who just shouldn't be allowed on the roads. Having said that, I know there are some cyclists who shouldn't be let on the roads as well.

That last Thursday Chris and I had a good relaxing evening together, enjoying one another's company as it would be the last time for a few days that we would be together. We had planned in our schedule that when we were passing through the area on our way south, we would each spend the night at home to recharge our batteries and set us up for the second half of the journey.

Before we went to bed, we packed my stuff, during the previous months I had acquired additional equipment. An extra helmet, additional shorts, shoes, cycling tops, gloves, sunglasses, energy drinks and numerous other items that I thought would be required during the trip.

I took an eternity getting everything ready, checking and double checking then just having another drink. I would do everything before going to bed because I knew that when I did as soon as I got to sleep the alarm would be going off before I knew where I was. Eventually the time had come, finally I had to stop prefabricating and get to bed otherwise I wouldn't be able to get up in the morning.

We went upstairs; I had a quick shower and jumped in bed, set the alarm and settled down. As I lay there I said a quiet prayer and then put my arm around Chris. I snuggled up to her enjoying the warmth of her body next to mine, as I started to relax my mind began to drift off, I could see John o' Groats, the old hotel on the headland, the little harbour and the fingerpost, the islands on the horizon, before long I had drifted off to sleep.

Chapter 3

Manchester to John o' Groats
THE GOOLY CHART, FIRST VIEWS OF THE ROUTE AND A LOVELY MEAL

As usual, it seemed that before I had got to sleep the alarm was going off. I woke and for a moment it just seemed like another typical Friday but then I remembered, today I was only working half a day, then I would be setting off for Scotland. I got up slowly and sat on the edge of the bed for a moment to pull myself together, I could feel the butterflies starting already in the pit of my stomach. Getting up off the bed I staggered to the bathroom, cleaned my teeth and went over to the shower and turned it on. After it had warmed up I stood under it and let the water pour over me. It was hot and relaxing and made me feel a bit better; I had a good long shower, shut it off, stepped out and got dried. I stood on the scales for the last time and looked down, 13 stone six pounds. I shook my head and felt the fat around my middle; it's no good worrying now I thought, you're going to have to carry this with you all the way pal.

I put a nice clean shirt on and got dressed in one of my usual work suits, I glanced out of the window; it was quite a decent morning, blue skies with the odd cloud drifting past. Good, I thought, not too much wind; I hope it stays that way. The wind is the worst of all options for me, the hills come to an end, the rain usually stops and doesn't make the cycling too difficult just unpleasant, but the wind can go on and batter you remorselessly and you never know when it's going to stop.

I had my normal breakfast of orange juice, two slices of toast and a cup of tea. When I had finished and relaxed for a while I decided it was time to set off for work. As I got in the car I lit a cigar and put the radio on, it was tuned in to Talk Sport as was usual. Driving down the familiar roads to work I started to wish I had booked the full day off, I thought, I'm never going to get any work done, I won't be able to concentrate on work this morning. It suddenly began to dawn on me how nervous I was; in fact, I felt like the condemned man the morning he goes to the gallows. For a long while I had anticipated the arrival of this weekend with a certain amount of trepidation, if not downright terror and now that long awaited and dreaded moment was almost upon me.

I got to work without really knowing how; I got on to the motorway and drove down to Urmston on auto pilot. Unfortunately for me, I had changed jobs since I had agreed to do the ride with Bill, so despite all Bill's fixing I wasn't getting the time off with pay from the firm after all, it had to come out of my holidays anyway. I must admit though, the construction firm where I was working at the time was one of the best places I had ever worked. They had a great team spirit and everyone was great fun yet hard working and very supportive of each other.

During the morning Dave, one of the real characters who worked in my office came in waving a large diagram he had drawn up. It had in large capital letters across the top, 'Fred's Gooly Chart', down the side it had the days of the week. It started on the Sunday, a block of four squares next to the day were coloured in pink and the colour got darker as you progressed down through the days to a deep purple on the following Sunday, which was when we were due to arrive. He pinned it on the wall and, of course, everyone in the office rolled around in laughter, they all thought it was highly amusing.

As it happened, a year or so later I got my own back on Dave when I talked him into walking Hadrian's Wall with me. After that experience he could hardly walk and he didn't play golf for a month. 'You've ruined my life you bitch' he swore at me.

'Remember the gooly chart?' I replied, 'We could have done one for your feet' I laughed, but that was far into the future and all I could do at the time was join in with the merriment.

The morning soon passed with most of my work colleagues popping into our office to wish me luck and quite a few subcontractors who had been good enough to sponsor us phoning in to wish us well. So before I knew where I was it was lunch time and time to head home. I left the building with excitement starting to build up inside me, I had been fine while I was at work with my friends and having a laugh but now I was alone in the car I could feel the tension clawing away at my stomach.

Being lunchtime the motorway and roads home were reasonably quiet, I listened to Classic FM as I drove home leisurely smoking a cigar. Before I got home I stopped to fill the car with petrol, putting the receipt safely away in the glove compartment as the petrol money was the only cost we were going to take as expenses out of the sponsorship money we raised. After a nice steady run from Urmston along the M60 I got home to Hazel Grove about one o'clock.

As I walked through the door Chris was waiting for me, 'Hi sweetheart, how are you?' she asked.

'Great' I replied. Not really too sure whether I was feeling great or not under the circumstances. 'Now that I've finished work it's just a couple of hours before we set off and I have the big challenge before me.'

'What time will you be leaving?' She asked 'Will you want some lunch?'

'I'll just have a sandwich thanks, we will have a meal when we stop at the services tonight, I'll leave here about 4.30 to pick up John before going for the van.'

It had been decided that to enable us to get to John o' Groats in plenty of time on the Saturday, we would leave on Friday night and stay at Tebay services on the M6. There is a nice secluded caravan site at Tebay where I have stayed many times before on trips to Scotland. It's only a couple of hours from Manchester but it gets you a good start for the run up to Scotland the next day and just a short walk away there is a hotel where you could get a half decent meal.

I spent the rest of the afternoon having a shower and relaxing as best I could, unfortunately whenever I tried to relax my stomach began to churn thinking of what lay ahead. So trying to keep my mind active I checked the equipment I had got ready the night before. After a further half hour I got up and checked my gear for what I said was to be the final time: and then I checked it again and again. Finally, when I was convinced I had everything and I couldn't delay any longer we packed the gear and loaded the two suitcases onto the back seat of the car. One which contained my cycling gear the other my evening clothes. I took the wheels off the bike and put it in the boot along with the spare wheels, inner tubes, tyres, bottles etc.

No matter how much I messed about the time finally arrived when I had to set off, Chris walked to the car with me. 'Be careful' she said.

'I will' I answered, it was the same thing we said to each other every time I went out on my bike. The familiarity of it made me feel a bit more at ease. 'I'll see you soon.' I said.

'I'll miss you', she replied. I gave her a kiss and at that moment I would have given everything I possessed to be able to go back in and cuddle up to her and not have to do this.

'I love you, look after yourself' I whispered to her.

'You look after yourself' she replied.

I turned and got in the car, she stood at the door and waved as I pulled out onto the road and drove away. God bring me home safely, I said to myself as I drove down the road towards the motorway.

I was really beginning to feel the pressure now I was on my own, so I turned the radio on to the Talk Sport channel, I thought I would listen to something light hearted and amusing to occupy my mind. I lit up a cigar and relaxed driving along nice and steadily in the late afternoon sunshine. As I drove through the, by now busy, Friday afternoon traffic along the M60 listening to the chatter on the radio and enjoying my cigar, my mind started to go through what it would be like on Sunday. My thoughts then turned to Bill; he won't be thinking of this, he will be happily oblivious of what is to come, I thought somewhat enviously.

Having driven round the M60 I came off at Bury went through the town and up to Brandelsholme to pick John up. It was just about 5.30 when I arrived at John's; he was watching for me and was at the door as I backed up the drive.

'Hi Fred' he called 'Are you all ready?'

'I could do with another month or two but I suppose I'm as ready as I will ever be.' I answered.

'Coming in for a brew before you set off?' he enquired.

'Yes that would be nice; it will be getting late before we get another chance.' I went in and sat down in the kitchen dining area, Christine, John's wife, was there brewing up.

'Tea or coffee?' she asked. I had a coffee and a biscuit. As I sat drinking my coffee Christine chatted about the ride, she was looking at me as if to say God Fred, you should have more sense than doing something like this at your age and if she had said it just at that moment I can tell you I would have been inclined to agree with her. We finished our drink and loaded John's gear onto the backseat of the car next to mine and then we were off to the compound where I kept the van.

When we arrived John got out to unlock the two pairs of double gates that led to the compound and I drove in; I pulled up in front of the caravan and got out of the car. 'Right John, let's get this show on the road' I said, I opened the boot and walked over to the caravan, my stomach was in knots as I switched our gear including the bike from the car to the caravan. I got a couple of posters out of the car that Cancer Research UK had given us, on which we had had printed, 'John o' Groats to Land's End bike ride in eight days' and stuck them in the van windows. We connected the battery, got everything sorted and wound up the legs. John backed the car up and we hitched it up and connected the electrics, as he drove the car and van outside the compound I stayed behind to lock the gates behind him.

At last, it was time to get on the road, I got in the passenger seat, John stayed behind the wheel and we set off, we were on our way. We drove along the A58 to Bolton, went around the ring road and then got on the M61 at Horwich. Going up the M61 we had arranged to meet Bill at the Bolton West services, it was about 7 o'clock when we arrived.

We sat there for about five minutes, I was feeling nervous so I got out, lit a cigar and stretched my legs using the excuse that we would be stuck in the car for a while. We must only have been waiting there about 10 minutes when a car drove on to the car park and pulled across to us, it was Gill and Bill. They drove over to the van and pulled up, Bill jumped out of the car, he was all smiles. 'Great day to set off on our adventure' he said, with a big grin on his face.

Walking about on the car park waiting for them had given me time to start dwelling again about what was in front of me and my stomach had started churning. I was itching to say 'Well bl**dy well enjoy it while you can, because on Sunday that smile will be wiped off your smug face', but I kept my counsel and just smiled back at him and said 'Yes it will be a pleasant trip up if it stays like this.'

We transferred Bill's gear and bike into the van, Gill and Bill said their goodbyes then he got in the back of the car and we were on our way. The miles soon started to tick away as we cruised up the M61 then the M6. Bill was full of himself and kept the idle chatter up as we drove along, I was more subdued but whether either Bill or John noticed I don't know, if they did, they didn't say anything.

Despite quite a bit of heavy traffic at this time, we soon passed the Preston turn off, heading up the motorway to the Tebay services. I don't know if you've been there but the caravan site is surprisingly very good, as you go along the slip road to the services there is a left turn that drops quite steeply down. This leads down to the campsite, it must be 10 metres below the level of the motorway and totally surrounded by trees. Therefore, once you get down to where you pitch the vans you can't hear the traffic on the motorway as the sound is not only absorbed by the trees but also goes straight over the top.

We pulled up outside the office and went in to book in and get our pitch number. Having signed in and paid we drove down and located our pitch, John backed the caravan on to it and as we were only staying the night we didn't unhitch the van, we just put the back legs down. I went to get some water in the barrel and John connected the waste while Bill set up his tent at the back.

We brewed up and relaxed for half an hour then we set off to the hotel for our evening meal. It was about nine o'clock and still light as we walked up the path to the hotel. I lit a cigar and in the fading light as we walked along, all I could think of were the days ahead and what we would have to go through. Bill, meanwhile, was as happy as Larry, he hadn't a clue and he didn't have a care in the world. God! How I envied him.

We got to the hotel, made our way into the restaurant and sat on the nice comfortable settees. John ordered the drinks, Bill had a pint of lager and John and I had a gin and tonic each, Bill and I lit a cigar while we studied the menu.

I lay back on the settee enjoying my cigar while I poured over the menu and wondered what Chris was doing at that moment. No doubt she would be watching the television and possibly wondering what I was up to, I got my phone out and gave her a ring as I had promised I would each night. The conversation was short and sweet, it was only a few hours since I had left so there wasn't much to say apart from that we had a good journey and got set up OK for the night.

The waiter came in and we ordered our meals, as it was late I just had a light meal and we ordered a glass of wine each instead of a bottle. We were getting up at six o'clock in the morning and had a long day ahead of us so we didn't want a heavy night.

The meal was quite good as far as it goes and we had a pleasant relaxing evening. 10.45 we were on our way back to the van, I lit a cigar and as we strolled along the lane back to the site I looked up at the sky. There wasn't a cloud in the sky and with it being late in July it was quite dark by then. We made our way to the caravan, Bill went straight to his tent and John and I got the sleeping bags out in the caravan. Within 10 minutes we were both asleep, it had been a long day since I got up for work at 5.45 that morning and the nerves had begun to tell. I slept like a log, no doubt thanks in no small part to the late meal and the couple of gin and tonics.

We woke up early next morning, the sun was already shining on a beautiful day, I looked through the caravan window and the rabbits were grazing and running about all over the site. It was one of those days when you felt great to be alive, I called John but he was already awake, 'Time to get up mate,' I said, 'It's a fabulous morning, great for a run up to Scotland.'

He sat up and looked through the window. 'It certainly is,' he replied as he rubbed his eyes 'what great conditions for travelling.'

We got up and woke Bill, showered, had a quick breakfast and packed up the van and tent; we were on the road by 7 o'clock.

We soon got up the motorway with John and I taking it in turns to drive, the M6 was followed by what was then a short stretch of the A74 and then the A74M, stopping for some lunch at Abington services about 30 miles from Glasgow.

As it happens the services at Abington are just off the motorway and the route we were going to take from John o' Groats to Land's End goes along the road and past the services.

'Just think Bill' I said 'In four days' time we will be cycling through here.'

'Great, I can't wait to get going' he says, smiling with thrilled anticipation.

You won't think it's great by the time we get here I thought, but I left him to enjoy his ignorance for the time being.

We carried on, the traffic getting heavier, we then transferred onto the M73 up the east side of Glasgow. Soon it changed to the A80 through Cumbernauld and then the M80 followed by the M9 heading towards Stirling. From Stirling we got onto the A9 and from there it was a fast road which bypasses Perth and on past Pitlochry through some lovely scenery past Dalwhinnie and Kingussie where you can see the impressive remains of Ruthven Barracks to your right. After the 1715 Jacobite uprisings the British Government built four fortified barracks in strategic locations in Scotland to help quell any insurgencies, Ruthven Barracks was one of them. It stands isolated on the top of the hill and it looked huge, black and forbidding against the blue sky as we drove past.

Along this length, the A9 is passing along the northern edge of the Cairngorm National Park, so all along to the south are fabulous views of majestic mountains. Shortly afterwards, we passed through Aviemore and then it was direct north again and on to Inverness.

Once we had passed through Inverness we were on the actual route we would be coming down the next day so I was fascinated, looking out of the window and taking it all in. Bill was totally relaxed and chatting, I don't think it ever entered his head that he would be cycling down this road the next day.

We started out of Inverness across the Black Isle, the hill at the North side heading down towards the bridge over the Cromarty Firth is a beast and this would be the last major climb on our first day. I watched with apprehension as we went down and down the hill towards the bridge, it seemed to go on forever. I didn't comment about it to Bill, I thought what he didn't know couldn't hurt him, at least not until tomorrow when he was faced with the prospect of climbing it with over a hundred miles in his legs.

We drove along the Firth towards Invergordon, in the distance at the mouth of the Firth we could see several giant oil drilling platforms. Whether they were moth balled or what I don't know, but from where we were you could tell they must have been massive structures.

The road turned north again and we headed away from Cromarty Firth and started to head for the Dornach Firth. We went across the bridge at the mouth and soon we were on the coast heading for Brora and on to Helmsdale. As we passed through Helmsdale I lit a cigar and sat back watching the scenery.

I knew what was coming up; between Helmsdale and just after Berriedale there are two long hard climbs one after the other that I remembered from the first time I had cycled through. As we went over them, I remembered vividly the effort required getting up them but Bill never even noticed, he was too busy talking to John.

Twenty miles after Helmsdale we came to a place called Latheron where the road branches, the A9 goes left heading for Thurso, it's here you finally take your leave of the A9 and take the A99 that you will follow all the way to Land's End. I have been to many places in my life, some of which have left an indelible impression on me, like the Cote D'Azure in the summer. Driving leisurely along that coast in the sunshine is out of this world. But, to me, the North East coast of Scotland on a lovely day is just as beautiful and I can tell you this for nothing, it's a damn sight pleasanter to drive along. Anyone who has driven along the Riviera in the summer will know what I mean.

The remainder of the trip followed the coast and with the sun shining and the sea beautiful shades of blue, it was just so relaxing and memorable, I sat back, lit a cigar and enjoyed every minute of it. Unfortunately, as I realised we were getting closer to our destination, I started to think it was a pity I wouldn't be able to enjoy it quite the same tomorrow.

I don't know what it is, but whenever I have travelled north to John o' Groats, as I get nearer the town itself I always have this feeling that I am running out of land, that there's nowhere else to go. It's a strange feeling really because having been down to Land's End on many occasions I never get the same feeling there. Possibly it's due to the fact that the landscape is much more barren and there are fewer houses and villages than there are in Cornwall.

We arrived at John o' Groats at exactly 5.15 that evening, it was 516 miles on the clock from when we started, for those people interested in such details. I know this because, as I say, John was extremely organised and kept a detailed log of our trip. It had been a fabulous day all the way up and the sun was still shining in a perfect blue sky.

We went to the office at the campsite and booked in for the night. After pitching our caravan we put up Bill's tent, and inflated his blow up bed. It was then we found he had lost the stopper from the valve; he must have dropped it that morning when we were packing up at Tebay. After much cussing and swearing he had to sit holding the nozzle to stop it going down while we searched for something to replace the stopper. After a lot of rooting around we found a small piece of wood, shaped it with a knife out of the van and wedged it in the valve. Having got the van and, finally, the tent set up we all phoned our respective partners to let them know that we had arrived safely.

Chris was thrilled to hear from me and glad to know that everything was alright; she said it had been a lovely day in Manchester as well but apparently the weather forecast for the following day was not too brilliant. 'Well we are a long way from you so hopefully it won't be too bad up here.' I replied.

'I'll phone the kids and keep them informed if you want then you won't have to spend half of each night on the phone.' She said.

'Yes that's a good idea; I don't know what time I'll be phoning, it'll probably be about seven to 7.30.' I replied.

'Right have a good night's rest and take care tomorrow, I'll be thinking of you.' She whispered quietly.

'I love you.' I answered then I hung up.

We all unpacked our gear and then decided to have a walk down to the centre which was about two to three hundred yards away. For those of you who have never been, it's a lovely little place especially in nice weather. There's not much there, a little souvenir shop, a cafe bar, the campsite, a small harbour and a magnificent derelict boarded up hotel with fantastic turrets. It's the sort of place that if I had been a lot younger and won the lottery I would love to buy and restore then try to make a success of it.

We called in The Last Shop in Britain and discovered that they had 'John o' Groats to Land's End Record' cards. Apparently when one does a John o' Groats to Land's End you are intended to get them filled in on the way down at certain places. I must admit we did not bother as they have to be stamped at various shops or hotels that partake in the scheme and we didn't fancy searching them out on the way down.

Having got our cards we strolled back to the van, got the folding chairs out and sat outside the van with a gin and tonic each. Stretched out on our chairs Bill and I enjoying a cigar, John, who didn't smoke, just relaxing as we watched the ships plying their trade between the islands and the mainland to the most southerly of the Orkney Isles. It was a memorable, beautiful evening as we relaxed enjoying the sunshine. It was so pleasant as I sat there soaking it all in, I knew it would be the last totally relaxing, comfortable night for eight days and I intended to enjoy it to the full. After a short while we all shaved, showered and got changed, feeling fresh and relaxed we sat outside the van; the evening was everything we could have asked for.

The site for July was really quiet, the evening was perfect, the clouds white and fluffy, the temperature warm, if you didn't know about the horrors that were to follow the next day it would have been quite idyllic. After a relaxing hour we strolled up the road leading out of the village for about half a mile to The Sea View Hotel for dinner. At least the initial preparation for this trip was working out far better than the last time I had done it. Then we didn't leave until Saturday morning, I had to pick the others up at Preston so we didn't arrive until 10.30 at night and we couldn't get anything to eat anywhere, we finished up with a packet of crisps each from the local pub.

This time we all settled into our seats in the restaurant, enjoyed a gin and tonic while we perused the menu at our leisure. I decided on Moules Marinière to start followed by a nice rare rump steak, chips and vegetables. As we all had the steak we ordered a bottle of Châteauneuf-du-Pape to help it down, followed by cheese and biscuits, coffee, brandy and cigars (for Bill and I). Not perhaps what you might see recommended in the best training manuals but very nice thank you.

After a very enjoyable evening meal, where even I managed to relax and put the thoughts of tomorrow out of my head for a while, we then had a quiet stroll back down to the caravan and Bill to his tent for a relatively early night.

I stood outside the van and pulled a last cigar out of the packet, lit it and took a long pull on it, feeling the smoke going down. I exhaled deeply and looked up into the heavens. The stars were twinkling brightly; there was a lovely crescent moon. It was wonderful; you could see thousands more stars here than you could at home without the street lights and the light from Stockport masking them. When I was young, astronomy was my hobby, so I took the opportunity of revisiting some constellations that I had not seen for years. I then looked out to sea and watched the twinkling lights of the ships and the houses on the nearest island which I took to be Stroma.

I stood there enjoying the cigar deep in thought, after a while my mind drifted to tomorrow and I was then brought back to reality thinking about the next morning, imagining going back along the road we had just come up a few hours ago. After several minutes John called me. 'Got a coffee for you here Fred if you're ready.'

'Right' I called, 'Thanks.' So I finished my cigar had a last look at the lights and stars so as to fix them in my mind, thought about Chris at home and wondered if she was in bed then went in to get ready for bed.

I turned the main light off in the van and switched on the small one over my bed, got into the sleeping bag feeling nice and cosy and drank my coffee, 'Good night' I said but John was already asleep. So I turned the light off and settling down I thought about Chris again back at home alone, sensing that she would be thinking of me. I said a prayer and just remember thinking; tomorrow the story begins, as I fell asleep.

Chapter 4

Day 1 John o' Groat's to Inverness
THE FIRST OF THOUSANDS, SOD THEM BRAES AND VERTIGO!

The alarm went off at 6.30. As is often the case at first, I wondered where I was. Then the cold reality set in and I remembered what was in front of me, I suddenly thought oh no! The day I have been waiting for, dreading and hoping would never come, has finally arrived. I raised myself on my arm and knocked the alarm off, John was starting to move on the bed on the other side of the caravan.

'This is it' I said in a not too convincing voice, 'We go into another world for the next eight days.'

'Don't worry,' he replied sleepily, 'everything will be fine, you can do it.'

'No, we can do it' I said, 'This is a team effort, it will take us all working together, a lot of luck and God's help to get us to the other end.'

I raised the blind a bit and looked out of the window, the sunshine of the previous day had not completely gone, it was a bit cloudier but there was still plenty of blue sky and at least it wasn't raining. Getting up I had a quick wash in the van, got into my shorts and chose a blue top. I like the yellow tops usually as I think they are very distinctive when you are cycling and car drivers can see you better but as the roads would be quiet today I thought I would save the yellow for later. I put on my socks but with just my slippers for the time being, walking around in cycling shoes with cleats on is no fun I can tell you.

I went outside and walked round to Bill's tent, unzipping it I called gently so as not to disturb other campers nearby. Bill began to stir in his tent; he got up and five minutes later joined us in the caravan for breakfast. It wasn't anything fancy considering it's supposed to be the most important meal of the day: John had toast, Bill and I had cereal and then it was, have your hot drink and get ready for the ride. This, I thought, is going to be our life now for the next eight days. We filled our water bottles, this first day Bill actually used a pack, which was a soft plastic container that strapped to his back which he filled with water and sucked from a tube that came across the front of him. I stuck to the traditional bottles; I filled half my bottles with an energy drink and the other half with water. I knew if I filled them all with energy drink I would be chewing the damned stuff to get it down by the end of the day.

I went out to the car and opened the boot, got my bike out and quickly put the wheels on, slipped two bottles into the cages, one of each and put the other eight in the boot of the car. I checked my back pockets to make sure I had my energy bars, dextrose tablets, spare inner tubes and puncture repair kit, some cash and most importantly a full packet of cigars and a lighter.

Bending over I checked the tyres, I straightened up and looked around me, the islands were still there, the other caravans, nothing had changed since last night except for us. I looked south in the direction we would be going and thought of all the people still asleep in bed on the site, they will just get up and continue with their life very much as they did yesterday. They are all on holiday, it's a Sunday morning, some may be going home, some may have just arrived like us, but probably none of them are going to have such a complete change of life for the next eight days as Bill, John and I.

One good thing about having John on board was, unlike the last time I did this, at least we didn't have to pack the caravan up, empty the waste, store everything away, raise the feet, hitch it up and all that before we left. All we had to do was to take Bill's tent down, being a caravaner himself, John would pack the caravan and hitch it up on his own when we had set off. Soon Bill had set up his bike, we both had another quick trip to the toilet (about the third that morning) and then there was nothing else to do. It was time to go, I was nervous and apprehensive, Bill all excited and looking forward to it. I kicked off my slippers in the van and slipped my cycling shoes on, John locked the van door as we left and we set off down the road clattering on our cleats pushing our bikes down to the finger post.

The finger post for those who don't know is the sign that says John o' Groats and shows the distance to Land's End and other places, if you want they can put the nearest place to your home town on with the mileage. As it happened it was far too early in the morning for the photographer to be there, so we just made do with taking our own photographs without our home towns on the post. Unfortunately for people who do this ride in the future, they will be unable to set off as early as we did and take their own photographs at the post. As the last time I was up there, we were talking to the guy with the franchise for taking the photographs and due to constant vandalism he now has a post he can take away at the end of the day. It's a shame but unfortunately it seems to be the way the world is going these days.

We pushed our bikes along the few hundred yards or so, with John walking alongside us carrying his camera. The sun was in and out, dodging behind clouds but there was quite a bit of blue sky which always makes me feel better if I am setting off on a long bike ride.

As we went past the car park we noticed there was a large coach parked up on the coach park with a long trailer attached to it. All along the trailer in three horizontal rows was a line of windows approximately two foot square. After we had left, John found out that they were little individual bedrooms for the people on the coach. It was full of tourists from somewhere in Europe having a cheap holiday touring Britain and this was their accommodation.

When we arrived, Bill and I climbed up onto the little pedestal to pose at the fingerpost for the obligatory photographs, we jumped down and standing astride our bikes had more photographs taken. Then we all shook hands and wished each other luck, little did Bill realise at that time how much we would need it, I had learned the hard way from the last time I had done this, when the preparation I had put in was totally inadequate for the trip. This time, though I had put more miles in, it was in shorter runs rather than longer distances, so we still were not fully prepared and I was also a few years older.

During the training for the ride I had never done more than 65 miles and that only seven or eight times. I had never got anywhere near doing a 110 miles: then another the day after, but that was what we were going to have to average for the next eight days.

I looked at my watch, it was 7.50. Bill was raring to go and full of optimism, I was apprehensive and, to be quite honest, feeling a bit sick. I was the only one who knew the full extent of what was before us and I knew that the work we had put in was not going to be anywhere near enough for us to complete the ride comfortably. But, whatever we had done or should have done or could have done, that was all in the past, now it was time to stand up and be counted, 873 miles of road lay stretched out in front of us. I looked at Bill; he looked relaxed and was smiling. I thought to myself, you may be smiling now lad, but if you knew what was in front of you I can tell you now, you would get off that bl**dy bike, walk back, put the tent up and go back to bed.

We straddled our bikes ready to go but for a second or two, it was as if the whole world stood still. I was in a trance looking up the road, John and Bill didn't exist, I felt like I could blink and I would be back home with Chris and it would all be a bad dream.

I don't know how long I stood there: it seemed like ages, then slowly I started to come round, I became aware of a seagull calling overhead, it brought me back to reality. I looked up at it soaring above in the blue sky among the puffy white clouds, free and effortless and felt a pang of envy. It started screeching again sounding for all the world as if it was laughing at us, it probably was.

Looking back up the road I gripped the handlebars, jammed my right cleat into the pedal and pushed down, slipping my left foot into the other pedal and I was off. Bill immediately followed, I turned and with a cheery wave to John shouted, 'See you down the road somewhere,' and our legs did the first few rotations of the countless thousands that they were going to do over the next eight days.

It was almost 7.55, later than I would have liked, but we confidently set off up the short climb from the finger post. By the time I had reached the top of the rise I was breathing heavily but that was natural for me until I got my second wind. We went past the Seaview Hotel where, fewer than 12 hours ago, we had had such a lovely relaxing meal. A road branches off just opposite the hotel, the A836 passes the Castle of May which used to belong to the Queen Mother but now belongs to Prince Charles, then goes on to Castletown and Thurso. If you're ever up that neck of the woods the castle is well worth a visit, a bit dour perhaps and not furnished to my taste but the gardens are lovely.

As I got into my rhythm, it seemed as if it was yesterday when I had set off down this road before, the four years seemed to have just melted away. We started at a rather slower pace than we intended to average trying to get into our stride. I remember thinking as we set off, at least the weather is better than the last time, then it had been a dull and grey day.

The A99 out of John o' Groats is a slight climb which rises just over 300ft in the first two and a half miles, once you get on the top it reminds me of what I imagine the Russian tundra looks like. It's wild and barren, not a tree or hill as such in sight, it gives you the impression it goes on forever and it's all under a massive sky.

The cross wind we were pedalling against was making life a bit uncomfortable, not as bad as I had remembered but still strong enough to reduce our comfortable 16 miles per hour to a hard 14. This makes all the difference when you are going to cycle 125 miles in the day like we had to do today. It could add another one and a half hours onto your day, which is a long time in the saddle when you have been out 10 hours.

We were soon cruising along and I was beginning to enjoy it despite myself, after about six miles we saw a guy walking up the road towards us, carrying a door. We commented on this as we hadn't passed a house for about two miles and as far as we could see there were no houses in view. (Some weeks after, we got an End to End magazine which had a photograph of a guy who had walked from Land's End to John o' Groats carrying a door. Well, as I said at the beginning, there are a lot of nutcases in this world, though he was carrying it to raise money for cancer research in memory of his father who had been a joiner, so good on him.)

After approximately 50 minutes we were at a small place called Reiss where the road hits the B876 and you turn left to head into Wick. If you turn right here on the B876 you head north to Castletown on Dunnet Bay which to my mind has one of the most beautiful beaches in the country. Bill was still relishing the run and enjoying every minute.

You may have noticed when you look back on projects you have been involved in, things always seem like a good idea when you're sat at home in the warm, discussing them over a drink or two. When you get to the cold light of day, however, it doesn't seem such a brilliant idea after all. Well I can tell you, this didn't even seem a great idea to me when I was sat at home in the warm. So now feeling every bump in the road and the constant wind in your face knowing you've done 15 miles in the first hour and thinking of the distance we were going to cycle, not only today but for the next seven days and how far it was to Land's End, well I can tell you it really starts to get to you, well it did me anyway.

Three to four miles after Reiss we were in the outskirts of Wick, a major place up this neck of the woods but a small town to us. Despite there being only one major road through the town we managed to take the wrong turning at a roundabout and finished up cycling along the harbour front. It was really picturesque with the tide in and the colourful fishing boats bobbing up and down but it was a diversion we could well do without.

'For Pete's sake!' Bill called out, as I pulled up overlooking the harbour wall. 'I thought you'd done this once.'

'I just wanted to see where it led to, that's all, no need to get uptight.' I answered, 'Everything's under control, we'll just cycle back to the roundabout now.'

We turned around and headed back, it only took a couple of minutes but just as we were approaching the roundabout to get back onto the A99 we saw John sailing past with the caravan. Unfortunately, this meant our support vehicle which was supposed to be behind us most of the time, was now in front and obviously not having seen us John didn't realise this.

'What are we going to do?' Bill asked, 'Shall we stop and phone him?'

'No' I replied as we pedalled on, 'It won't take him long to realise he's passed us, then he'll pull up in the first layby he comes to.'

Sure enough, half an hour later there he was, sat in a layby waiting for us. We pulled over and took the opportunity to have a short break; we got off the bikes, leaned them up against the caravan and lit a cigar each. 'Thought you were doing well,' he said as we strolled up to the car. 'What happened to you?'

'Technical hitch' I replied, 'In a one street town we took the wrong street, finished up looking at the fishing boats down by the harbour.'

'Great,' John replied 'You've gone all of 17 miles and gone wrong already.'

'Just fancied a bit of sightseeing' I replied.

'How do you think you're doing?' he asked.

'So far so good, just got into the groove now, don't want to stop too long, we'll just finish the cigars and get on the road again, save us stiffening up.'

'How are you Bill?' John asked looking across at him.

'No problems so far, but then again we haven't started yet.' Bill answered.

'I will let you get half an hour to an hour's start on me before I set off.' John said.

'Right then, see you later' I shouted as we got back on our bikes and set off down the road.

As I began to get into my rhythm, I started to feel better about the challenge, I was feeling good in myself and began to think, yes, this is the life, pushing yourself to see what you are made of, let's get down this road as quick as we can. Although I knew there were three relatively hard climbs, it was probably going to be easier than tomorrow.

After Wick, the road was really quite fast, all long sweeping bends and gentle undulations. We were soon back into our stride again and making good time. Before long we went past a signpost that said Inverness 106 miles. Bill looked across at me, 'Doesn't sound far if you say it fast,' he said.

I smiled, 'See that other place Helmsdale 37 miles,' I said, Bill nodded. 'When you get there you've got two thirds of the day's major climbs behind you. You can relax then for about 40 miles until you get to the 'Black Isle' and by that time the end's in sight.'

I must admit as you ride down the A99 and also after Latheron when it changes to the A9 it must be one of the most beautiful roads in the country, the views inland are not all that fantastic at times but the coastal views are stunning. It was mile after mile of quiet countryside, blue skies with occasional cloud but looking out to the coast and across the sea was fantastic. If I have said it before I make no apologies for repeating myself, but apart from the Highlands the scenery along this coast is some of, if not the finest along the whole route.

As we got to about the 40 mile mark we started to climb, nothing desperate but a long, long climb. Over three and a half miles, it goes from 100ft above sea level to 500ft. I was just about shattered when I reached the top, I looked across at Bill, and he looked just as bad. 'I'm glad that's over with' he gasped.

'By the way, should you happen to get in front of me, brake hard before the bottom as there is a wicked hairpin, don't want you going over the edge without any wings' I called to him as we started to go over the top.

Having warned him I thought I would try to make sure he didn't get in front of me, I dropped several gears and standing up on the pedals I started to drive down the other side dropping gears until I was on the smallest cog and the cycle computer was registering almost 40 miles per hour.

The descent drops down inside a mile and a half into what is known as the Berriedale Braes. Bill followed me, I usually went downhill faster than him, partly due to my weight but also because Bill wasn't as confident on the downhill sections as I was. As I approached the bottom I started to brake, by the time I was turning into the first hairpin I was going at a crawl.

Once at the bottom, you have arrived at Berriedale, an insignificant little village you'd think if you ever pass that way in a car. You would probably notice the hairpin bends but wouldn't even register the climb between there and Helmsdale. But I can tell you, and any end to ender on a bike will confirm my opinion, that following the earlier climb the one out of Berriedale is just one climb too many in close succession, it's absolutely shattering. Now you may think I'm exaggerating slightly regarding these hills and ok, they wouldn't be anything in Tour de France standard for professional cyclists, but for an overweight 54-year-old they don't come a lot worse and if they did, if you had any sense you wouldn't go up them I can tell you.

We negotiated the first hairpin no trouble and as we came out of the second we shot down the road, past the memorial on our right-hand side. The climb out of the valley starts as soon as you reach the bottom. For a couple of hundred yards it's gradual, but then it really racks up. The first three quarters of a mile or so average about a 10 per cent gradient with parts around an 18 per cent incline and I can tell you, I was soon on the biggest gear at the back and my legs and lungs were really letting me know what they thought of it. As we started the climb I began to think of the last time I had done this, when I couldn't stop the thought going through my mind that I'd never finish the first day let alone nine days. This time, however, though I still felt the effort, I knew I had done it once and I was confident I would do it again.

I didn't try to get up as fast as I could; I just stuck in that bottom gear and got a steady rhythm going to get me to the top. As we struggled up the first slopes I looked across at Bill who was in front of me and thought, I hope you're having your doubts now my mate and if you're not, just wait till you get halfway up. I had a quiet smile to myself as I imagined how he was oblivious of what was in front of him. I clenched my teeth and shut myself away in that little room inside my head that I retreat to when the struggle gets too much, where there is no pain or suffering just numbness. I sensed my body as if at a distance, grinding on and on in bottom gear, my gasping breath sounded as if it was a long way away. I started to imagine what was going through Bill's mind, I imagined him thinking like I did the first time, that every bend you got round you would see the summit, but every time you got round the road went on forever upwards.

As the hill went on the sweat was running off me and my legs were trembling trying to push the gears round. At every second I felt that I could get off and walk but I knew I had to keep cycling. I no longer thought about Bill, I just kept my head down and kept pushing those pedals round, how he was feeling was his problem; I had enough of my own to worry about without bothering about him.

Eventually, after what seemed an eternity, we finally got to what Bill thought was the top, as we crested the hill he rode straight off onto a grassy verge, got off his bike and collapsed on the grass at the side. 'Bl**dy hell' he gasped, 'I'm absolutely knackered let's have a cigar.' Although I was exhausted myself I couldn't help an inward smile and feeling of satisfaction. Serves you right, I thought, I dropped my bike on the grass, pulled a packet of cigars out of my shirt pocket. As I sat down I carefully unwrapped the foil, stuck the packet back in my back pocket and lit up the cigar. 'What the hell was that?' He gasped as he lay on the grass.

'The Berriedale Braes.' I replied as I lay down on the grass.

'Well it doesn't sound much but I can tell you this for nothing, you can sod them Braes off, I've had enough of them.'

We lay on our backs on the grass looking up into the sky; I watched the clouds drift by and listened to the birds singing in the trees, the sunshine and the warmth felt so relaxing. As I drew long and slow on my cigar it felt amazing just lying there listening to the birds. I blew out the smoke and watched it slowly spiral up into the sky until the breeze caught it and whisked it away. It felt wonderful but I knew we couldn't stop long or our legs would begin to stiffen. Also, I knew that this wasn't the summit, from here it went downhill for a way and then kicked back up for another 200ft. I looked across at Bill who was lying there with his eyes shut; I thought it would be kinder not to tell him just then.

As soon as I had finished the cigar, even though I felt I could lie there forever, I got up and started to stretch. 'Come on Bill, let's be on our way, we've done 50 miles and we have another 75 to do.'

'Hope there's no more hills like that' he replied.

'Only one' I said, 'and that's near the end, so let's get going.'

'Inverness here we come' said Bill as he got back on his bike. I just nodded in agreement thinking, you haven't finished yet pal.

Apart from the short downhill stretch the hill finally climbs from just above sea level to about 750ft, which is a gradient of four per cent overall in five miles but with the cumulative effect of the distance we had done, the previous hill and the 18 degree slope at the beginning, it had really taken its toll. We cycled on up the rest of the climb, then down the long descent into Helmsdale. We seemed to have been going a lifetime, yet we weren't even halfway yet.

Helmsdale is a lovely little village set on the shore with a small picturesque harbour full of little fishing boats. We cycled through past the stone fronted Bannockburn Bar then the old white painted Belgrave Arms Hotel. How I would have loved to call in and have a pint but we had to push on, over the bridge past a large monument to the right and out of town along the coast.

The next place of note you come to is Brora, a place where I have since stayed on holiday in the caravan and it is a lovely little village, with a beautiful little harbour and a golf course, ideal for a base to explore the far north-east coast. Further down is Dunrobin Castle a fabulous, huge, fairy tale like castle. Unfortunately, you don't get a good view of it from the road but it is a wonderful day out. It's the home of the Earls and Dukes of Sutherland, dating from the 13th century with many of its rooms open to the public.

In fact, the whole east coast of Scotland up from Inverness is ideal for a quiet relaxing holiday, with wonderful scenery, fabulous walks, great beaches and lots of places of interest for both adults and children.

Travelling on we got to the Dornach Firth 82 miles from John o' Groats, this is one of several places where you are eternally grateful they have built a bridge across the estuary as it saves you countless miles if you had to go around. The scenery is wild and exposed but fortunately the weather was still fair as we went across the half mile long bridge with the firth to both sides of us and the North Sea out to the east.

The last half of the ride seemed to pass in a daze, it's as if after 60 miles it doesn't get much worse, you just get into a stupor and keep going. On the first day we came across several end to enders on bikes going in the opposite direction, some loaded down with that much luggage you wonder how the hell they were going to get up those hills we had just come through.

However, as the day progressed we began to feel the strain, it had been hard graft and we were heading for the 100 mile mark, which was 35 miles further than we had ever done in training. We were just about to pass through a little hamlet when we arrived at a crossroads with quite a large stone built church with a spire built on a slight rise to the left. Bill pulled in up the road to the left and dismounted.

'Shall we have a cigar break?' He asked, as I pulled up alongside him.

'Don't see why not.' I replied.

So we sat down, had a drink and lit a cigar each, looking round there were quite a few cars on the car park, some with ribbons on.

'Must be a wedding going on inside,' Bill commented, 'Some poor bu**ger being led to the slaughter.'

I laughed; Bill was displaying the usual chip on his shoulder. 'It's not always that bad Bill, you've just been unlucky. Anyway I reckon you'll be marrying Gill before long.'

'Now you are being stupid.' he replied.

Just as we finished our cigars and were about to set off, the doors of the church were thrown open. We could hear the familiar sound of Mendelssohn's *Wedding March* come booming out of the church organ as the photographer came backing out of church clicking away on his camera like there was no tomorrow.

He was followed a few seconds after by the happy couple; we had been stood watching for a few moments when one of the guests, I think it was the bride's father came down to talk to us. When he found out what we were doing he was thrilled to bits for some reason I couldn't understand and rushed off to tell the bride and groom. After a moment's discussion with the photographer, they walked down the slope to us and asked us would we mind if we had our photographs taken with them, bikes and all? We readily agreed feeling honoured that they wanted us to be part of their big day.

After the photographs were taken we wished them luck and set off on our way again.

'Well,' I said, 'I've heard of brides having their pictures taken with chimney sweeps before, but never with a couple of end to end cyclists.'

'Yes, well they'll need all the luck they can get.' Bill answered. I just carried on cycling; I'm not going there again I thought.

The scenery being so beautiful in places often helps and at times when you are sheltered from the wind it can even seem quite pleasurable. But now, later on in the day, the weather was changing: the sky was blackening and those moments were getting very few and far between, even the scenery wasn't what it had been.

As we cycled along the Cromarty Firth I realised we were getting near to the end of our first day. By now the wind was getting up, the sky had clouded over and things were beginning to look threatening. 'How long do you reckon Fred?' Bill asked.

'By my reckoning we have about 25 miles to do, so at the speed we are averaging and taking into account the hill over the Black Isle which in our weakened state will be quite difficult, probably another two hours.' I answered.

'God!' he cried, 'I'll be bl**dy glad when we get there.'

As we cycled along the firth we could finally see the bridge stretched across in the distance, just a couple of miles up the road. I can't tell you how glad I was to see it, I was sure that Bill was thinking the same. Just get across that, I thought then up that beast of a hill and it's downhill all the way from there.

As we swung around the roundabout and on to the bridge, I suddenly felt the wind really driving from the side, before I had gone very far I was in bottom gear and struggling to keep up any speed at all even along the flat bridge. I struggled on across the mile long bridge heartened by the sign at the beginning that said 'Inverness 14 miles'. Once over the bridge, you're onto the 'Black Isle' and the last big climb of the day comes into full view. You start up what you think is the longest hill you would ever cycle up, at least it feels like that after you've cycled 100 miles. Not as steep as the ones near Helmsdale but it goes on and on and on until you think your legs are going to come to a stop. 'Bl**dy hell Fred, I'm glad this is the last hill I'm just about finished.' Bill shouted back as he led up the hill.

I pushed on a bit and caught him up, I shouted back to him, 'Don't you believe it Bill, there's always another hill.'

It is, in fact, four miles by the time it levels off, it's only about three per cent gradient but it's enough, at this stage, to have you cursing as you slowly grind your way up. Just as we got over the top we saw John parked in a layby, he didn't have the caravan, just the car, we pulled over to him and took the opportunity to have another cigar. 'Hi lads you've not got far to go now' he smiled. 'I've just sited the van.' He gave us the directions; fortunately it was just on the way out of Inverness on the A82, the road we would be going down the following day.

Just as we were about to set off the long threatened rain started quite hard, we quickly got our waterproof tops on before setting off down the other side. 'I'll see you soon, will put the kettle on for when you arrive' John said as he got ready to set off.

'Bu**er the kettle get the bl**dy gin out.' Bill answered as John set off.

'Come on Bill,' I cried 'it's downhill now all the way to Inverness.' It would have been a great run, a 30 to 40 mile per hour downhill road but for two things, one, I was shattered and two, by now it was pouring down and the road was full of water which made going at speed with all the traffic about a bit problematic.

We arrived at the outskirts of Inverness and just before we got into the town Bill saw the Kessock suspension bridge that leads across the Beauly Firth into the town. He pulled over suddenly, I pulled in with him, 'What's wrong?' I cried.

'I don't like heights; I don't think I can get over that.' He turned and looked at me, 'I have vertigo' he said in a quiet voice.

'Bl**dy hell' I said staring at him, 'Vertigo!' I repeated as if I didn't understand what he was saying. 'Bl**dy hell Bill, if you don't like this, wait until you see the Erskine Bridge.'

I looked around me like somebody not right as if looking for divine intervention to help me, Gordon Bennett! I thought, what a bl**dy time to tell me he has vertigo. There was nothing I could think of, we had to get over the bridge so I just said 'Look, get onto my back wheel, keep your eyes on that and don't look left or right until I tell you.' He nodded in agreement but he didn't look too sure about it. I'll give him credit though, he did what I told him. But I can tell you, that short bridge seemed to take an age to cross, but we managed to get over and into the town.

Fortunately the rain had stopped as we started leaving Inverness. Following the road to the site was easy; the Bught Caravan Site just off the A82 in the direction of Fort William where we would be heading for tomorrow. We slowly cycled round the site until we found our car and van.

As we finally got off the bike I felt a surge of relief as we leant our bikes against the van, took our wet waterproofs off, staggered in and collapsed, it was just gone eight o'clock. John had three gin and tonics and three cups out ready to pour a brew when we arrived, the kettle was just boiling.

Bill got the car keys off John and went to get his tent and bag out of the car. We had the tent up in no time and were soon sitting outside with our drinks recuperating. After half an hour we went for a shower, got changed and sat and enjoyed yet another cigar and gin and tonic for 10 minutes outside the van. After we had finished our drinks we decided it was time to go and get some dinner, it was then that we discovered that Bill had locked the car keys in the boot of the car.

Day's Distance: 123 miles.
Cumulative Distance: 123 miles.
Day's Climbing: 3,720ft
Total Climbing: 3,720ft

Chapter 5

Day 2 Inverness to Nowhere?
BRAVEHEART, GIN AND TONICS, CIGARS AND A GOOD TRAINING REGIME

Great, this was all we needed, after cycling 120 miles and looking forward to a nice meal and an early night, there we were, stuck, unable to get in the car and not even able to get our water bottles out. After scratching our heads for half an hour or so, we decided to phone my breakdown cover. I can't complain about the service, in fairness the guy was with us in no time.

While we waited we phoned the girls to let them know we had arrived safely. Chris sounded really pleased when I phoned, I suppose it's alright for us knowing what is happening but when you are 500 miles away not knowing what's going on must be difficult. I explained to her about the car keys and said I would phone again in the morning to let her know what had transpired.

When the man from the breakdown company arrived he was a local Scot, not the dour type but a jovial guy and quite full of himself. We quickly explained our predicament; he looked us up and down, one after the other. You could see what he was thinking and it was probably something on the lines of, idiot Sassenachs like these shouldn't be let out on their own. However, he left us in no doubt that he, a direct descendant of William Wallace and the representative of the superior Scottish race would sort us useless peasants out, that it wouldn't be a problem and he would have us in our car in no time flat. His face broke into a large smile as he said, 'Don't ye be worrying yourselves about it now, I'll have ye in ye car in two shakes of a dog's tail, ye see if I don't. I have just the right piece of equipment to sort it.'

Going back to his van, he soon returned with a thin piece of wire about three feet long which he flourished about with great enthusiasm. 'Och ey, this will do the job be gad, ye see if it won't.' He said this with such confidence and in a tone of voice which filled you with total admiration for the miracles of modern engineering. He left us in no doubt that it was patently obvious that it was only going to be a matter of seconds before the car door was open.

'Ye see this ere wire,' he said waving it at us. 'I just have to bend this to the necessary shape, push it between the rubber seals in the door and push down on that there button on the centre console between the driver and passenger seats and bingo the doors are open.' He said it in such a straight forward matter of fact manner you thought God what was all the fuss about? I don't know whether it was naivety or just sheer optimism or his overpowering personality and charisma but I remember thinking, great, we should be sorted in no time. How wrong can you be?

At first everything seemed to be going well, he slipped the rod between the door and jamb and started directing it towards the door release button; just as he had predicted. After a bit of struggling at first, he had to withdraw it a couple of times and bend it slightly to get the angle he required, but soon it was heading towards the button.

'Och ey' he says, 'It's on its way now, yeel be in ye car in no time, ye see if ye not.' We all stood around peering through the car windows watching him with baited breath, until it was almost on the button, then once more he could not quite get it right. He pulled it out again blaspheming as he yanked it out. You could almost hear the gasps of disappointment from his small audience as we were all engrossed in this virtuoso performance. He bent the bar a touch more and slid it in again, it slowly, ever so slowly went towards the door release button, the tension was building up noticeably among us watching avidly through the car windows.

At that moment it was as if the success of our bike ride depended on this Scotsman and his little bit of wire. All the months of training, flogging your body up hills and through awful conditions, this last day all 125 miles of it, struggling up those hills, all would have been in vain if this bit of wire did not open that door.

The wire got closer and closer, without realising it I had started to hold my breath as it hovered over the button. I think he was building up the suspense for effect as he hesitated. Then all at once it was on the button and he pushed, I saw the button go down and immediately looked at the lock button in the top of the door expecting to hear the click and see it jump up, there was silence, nothing happened, nothing at all.

I suddenly realised I was desperate for a breath of air and gulped it in, in a long loud gasp that seemed to drain all the energy from me right down to my legs, the disappointment was crushing.

'Bu**er.' He said vehemently, 'It must a slipped off, I'll try again.' We all looked desperately at one another, we knew it hadn't slipped off but no one wanted to admit it. Then we settled back and watched again as he redirected the wire towards the button once more.

Slowly, slowly the piece of wire stretched out towards the button, though we all watched avidly we realised at the bottom of our hearts it wasn't going to work. We were right, again he got a positive connection on the button, we saw it depress but again nothing happened. He swore something under his breath, I'm not quite sure what but it sounded something like 'Hot digert the knoo the _____,' and he finally withdrew the wire.

Straightening up he looked round at us, we could tell by the look on his face he wasn't going to come up with any earth shattering ideas any time soon. The jovial confidant, 'I can sort this out in no time expert,' had suddenly been deflated, for all his state of the art, high tech equipment he couldn't get that bl**dy door to open. Bill and I lit a cigar, we all looked at him; he had been our great Scottish hope, I'll have you in here in no time he had said and we believed him, we were now waiting for him to produce the goods.

You could tell by his face the moment he regained his composure, 'Don't ye be worrying now' he says trying to look positive and determined, 'I'll come up with something, ye see if I don't.'

After racking his brain for what seemed like half an hour his face suddenly broke into a big smile. 'Right,' he says getting enthusiastic again. 'Behind that arm rest in the back there, is there a panel that ye can open to get into the boot?' I looked at him with a worried frown on my brow wondering what was coming next.

'Yes' I replied, 'But where's this taking us? We haven't got the key to get in the car to get at it and if we did we would be able to get in the boot anyway.' He smiled patiently at me like the master addressing a young child.

'Yes' he says enthusiastically. 'But,' he hesitated for effect before delivering the final earth shattering brainwave, 'If you can find a small child, break that back window and put the child through, it might be able to get its arm inside the boot and get the keys.'

You may think I'm winding you up, but as God is my witness it's what he suggested, you can't imagine where they get these people from. I stood there gobsmacked, it seemed ages before I gathered myself, I stared at him in total disbelief thinking he must be joking but his face was deadly serious. 'Err' I stammered for a second, 'Err, can we think about that one for a bit?'

'Ach by all means,' he says in his cheery Scottish voice. 'But a think that would be ye best option under the circumstances.' I looked around at the other two, John was nearly cracking up, I looked away quickly to avoid laughing myself.

Mr Breakdown Man had packed his precision door opening equipment into the back of his van, namely his bent piece of wire and shut the door. Now he had sorted our problem it was evident that he was going to leave it to us to abduct a small child and shove him through the back window. So we thanked him for his assistance and asked him if there was anywhere where we could get a bite to eat.

He suggested a pizza place not far down the road so Bill volunteered to get the pizzas and the guy very kindly drove him to the place and brought him back, so we managed to get a half decent meal and it was only about 10 o'clock.

Before he went though he also gave us the number of the local Rover garage for us to phone the next morning, should we decide not to use his great idea. So, although we weren't too overenthusiastic about his brainwave, we thanked him for his efforts and waved him off. He was a decent guy at heart and it had been very good of him to run Bill to the pizza place and back.

We brewed up, put the table up in the van and sat down to eat our dinner, 'Well that's a great start to our journey' Bill said, sounding really disheartened.

'Forget it' I said, 'we just have to get over it somehow, we will be alright when we phone the Rover dealer in the morning.' I tried to sound a lot more positive than I felt. 'In the meantime let's enjoy the meal and relax tonight knowing we've got the first day over with quite well and tomorrow's another day.'

After the pizzas we all sat back with a gin and tonic while Bill and I lit a cigar each. After the exertions of the day, us cycling and John being stuck in the car for the best part of 12 hours, we just put our feet up and relaxed for half an hour.

It was getting on for midnight when we settled down. I lay there thinking about what we were going to do tomorrow, then I realised my body was aching, not just my legs but my chest, my back and my arms. I said a quick prayer asking to be refreshed for the morning and that we would get things sorted out. I asked God to bless Chris and look over her while I was away, then as usual sleep overcame me before I had finished.

As there was little we could do we had decided next morning to take the opportunity to have a lie in. We were up about eight o'clock having breakfast and at nine o'clock we phoned the Rover garage. They informed us that with the car being less than 12 months old they had no blanks or patterns for the key, so they would have to send to Germany and it would take about three weeks to get replacements.

'Three bl**dy weeks!' Bill cried, 'I could walk it from Germany in three bl**dy weeks, so much for German efficiency.'

It was just what we didn't want to hear, after much discussion we decided the best course of action was to phone a friend of ours who worked for a large logistics company. We managed to get in touch with him about 10 o'clock. Dave was a great friend of John and I from the caravan club, our families had been on dozens of rallies together over the years. We explained our predicament and asked if the company he worked for could get my spare car key to Inverness and if so how long would it take?

Dave was always really helpful and by a fortunate twist of fate, that morning he was not far from where I lived. 'If I get round to your house and pick up the key by 12 o'clock we can have them to our agents in Inverness by 11 o'clock next morning.' He said.

'That's brilliant Dave; I will phone Chris and tell her you will be calling to pick them up.'

'Right, I should be able to get there by about 12 o'clock.'

Immediately we phoned Chris and told her what had happened and that Dave would be picking up the key before 12 o'clock so make sure she was in. When we had finished I looked at Bill and John, 'Well it would seem there is nothing left for it now but to relax and make the most of the day's rest.

However, losing a day would cause a problem with Chris and our friends Sandy and Dave who had booked a farmhouse for bed and breakfast the following Friday, Saturday and Sunday night in Cornwall to watch us arrive on the Sunday. Now with the day's delay it meant we would arrive Monday instead of Sunday and they would be going home on the Monday. I decided we would have to try and make up time and get there earlier on the Monday so they would still be able to see us arrive before they had to set off home.

We decided to go for a walk, have a look around and perhaps find somewhere to go for dinner that night, we walked through the site and past the leisure centre heading towards the town, the way we had cycled in the day before. It was a quite pleasant sunny day similar to the majority of the previous day, so I was beginning to regret the lost day's cycling.

We soon arrived at a small Co-op and a large fish and chip shop next to the Pizza restaurant Bill had been to the night before. After walking about half an hour we arrived at the Highland Council offices, in this time we hadn't seen as much as a pub so it was decided we would turn back and stroll in the opposite direction for a while.

As we got back and went past the turning to the caravan site the surroundings became a little more picturesque, with little white painted cottages leading up to a canal bridge. It was a swing bridge and as we stopped and leaned over looking up the canal to the south, there was quite a large steamer moored there, apparently used for cruises on Loch Ness. Bill and I lit a cigar each and we all leaned over the bridge for several minutes watching the small cruise boats going underneath it and up the Caledonian Canal.

We walked on over the bridge, past a caravan sales place and a garage on our right and the Torvean Golf Club to our left. Just past the garage we saw the Loch Ness House Hotel, a very impressive looking white painted building with extensions built on either side. At the far side of the hotel was a small sign saying 'The Copper Kettle Pub'.

'That looks promising,' John said as we walked up to the sign.

So we strolled down the lane at the side and went inside; as it happened the Copper Kettle pub was part of the large hotel, John ordered a round of drinks and we sat down and looked at the menu.

'Well looks good enough for me,' Bill said after he had studied the menu. 'I think it will be fine here tonight and it's only 10 minutes from the caravan, what more could you ask?' John and I agreed, so we settled down to enjoy our drinks and cigars.

After we finished our drinks we made our way back to the caravan, got the chairs out and the little table and set them up on the sunny side of the van. 'Look, what are our plans for tomorrow? If all goes to schedule I won't get the key until sometime about 11 o'clock. What do you two want to do?' he asked.

I had a drink of my gin and tonic then a pull on the cigar while I thought about it. 'Well,' I said slowly, 'We have two options. One, we can wait with you until you get the key and then set off which puts us another half a day behind after losing a day today. Or we can get up early as normal and set off; hoping that you get the key as planned, then you can catch up with us.'

'Yes that sounds alright, but what happens if he doesn't get the key?' Bill asked.

Now there was no way I wanted to lose another half a day so I replied. 'Well, all I can think of is that we take our credit cards and if the worst comes to the worst, we can get bed and breakfast in Crianlarich. Ok we wouldn't have any clothes or anything but we could get a shower and then we would have to set off the next morning again in the same gear and hope to God that the key arrives the next day.'

The three of us discussed all the possibilities at length, it must have taken about three gin and tonics each and Bill and I a couple of cigars before we finally arrived at the decision to carry on in the morning as I had suggested. The three of us were enjoying the sunshine when a chap from a caravan farther down the site came past. He stopped and looking at the sign on the window of the caravan which said 'John o' Groats to Land's End in eight days for Cancer Research UK.' He then looked down at us, sat sprawled out with our gin and tonics and cigars. 'Well lads,' he said as he looked us up and down, 'That looks like a bl**dy good training regime you lot have got there.' He then carried on along his way leaving us looking at one another unable to think of a reply.

About 6pm we all went to the shower block, had a shower, shaved and got changed ready to go out for dinner. We walked leisurely back up the road we had gone up earlier in the day, stopping at the bridge again for a few minutes watching the cruisers coming and going, then made our way to the Copper Kettle.

We settled down, got a round of drinks and made ourselves comfortable in the armchairs while we looked through the menu again. 'Do you fancy a bottle of wine?' Bill asked as we ordered our meals.

'No' I replied, 'I think we'd better just have a glass after all the drinks we've had this afternoon.' Bill agreed, so we each placed our orders and ordered a glass of wine each. The meal was excellent and though it had been a cock up of a day it had been quite pleasant, it was unfortunate that all our plans had been thrown into disarray.

With dining early we were soon back at the van relaxing and having a cup of coffee, I looked at Bill and John, 'Look, we want an early start in the morning and it's going to be a long hard day so I suggest we get to bed early tonight and get some rest.'

'It's alright with me,' John said, 'I won't be leaving until after 11 but by all means we might as well get the rest while we can.'

So Bill and I lit a last cigar each and strolled outside with our drinks in our hand, the caravan site was beginning to quieten down. 'Well!' Bill said as he looked pensively at the sky, 'I hope that key arrives in the morning or it will be fun and games.'

I looked across at him, 'I'm sure it will, if Dave said it would be there it'll be there, you can count on it.' I said, with a lot more confidence than I felt at the time but I didn't want anyone changing the plan. I was determined to get on the road early tomorrow and keep as near to the original programme as possible so we would get to Land's End while Chris was still there.

We finished our cigars, Bill said goodnight and gave me his cup as he climbed into the tent, I took it off him and went back in the caravan. We got the sleeping bags out from under the bunk, set the alarm clocks and climbed in. 'Have a good night,' I called to John.

'Just hope that the key is waiting for me when I get there tomorrow.'
He said as he settled down in his sleeping bag.

'Oh it will' I said again and shutting my eyes said a quiet prayer.

Day's Distance: 0 miles
Cumulative Distance: 123 miles
Day's Climbing: 0ft
Total Climbing: 3,720ft

Chapter 6

Day 2 (cycling) Inverness to Crianlarich
LOCHS, MOUNTAINS, COMMANDOS AND A STATE OF COLLAPSE

Day two (or is it three?) started with the alarm going off at six in the morning, we wanted to get an early start as it was to be another long day and definitely harder than the first. It looked quite reasonable weather wise but there was an uneasy feel to everything. Breakfast was quite subdued, as usual I had a bowl of muesli, Bill had cereal and John had his toast. We had got up early, and prepared to set off as we had agreed the night before, but beneath the surface we were all feeling very apprehensive about what was going to happen regarding the car key.

Anyway having decided on our plan of action the previous evening we set off at 7 o'clock, the only precautions we took was to take our credit cards and extra water bottles in our shirt pockets. I felt a bit stiff as we slowly cycled off the campsite but not as bad as I would have done without the day's break. We got back onto the main road and set off down the A82 towards Fort William, passing the little bridge and boatyard we had walked past the night before on our way to the Copper Kettle.

John had an easy morning and took his time packing up as he was going to make his way into Inverness to get to the depot for 11 o'clock to hopefully pick up the car key. We just prayed it would be there as, although we had our plans I don't think we were too keen about having to implement them. Our contingency plan of taking our credit cards with us, getting bed and breakfast somewhere if stranded without our back up and continuing the day after seemed OK when we had discussed it. However, we would have to find somewhere to stop and had no change of clothes or anything. So if there was a problem the next day and he still hadn't picked up the keys we would just have to keep cycling until John caught us up and it could get a bit problematic if there was a hitch.

To make things worse I started this day with a certain amount of trepidation as today we were to ride through Glen Coe. Now Glen Coe is my spiritual home, as a walker it is one of my favourite places, but as a cyclist it was something different again entirely. I was not looking forward to it with any great enthusiasm I can tell you. The last time I had done it, it was a nightmare, it rained most of the day and halfway up I dropped my drink bottle and had to stop to pick it up, getting started again afterwards was so incredibly hard I nearly gave up and walked up the damn glen.

Fortunately, the run from Inverness to Fort William is quite exhilarating as the road is very quiet, flat or gently undulating with lovely views across the loch from the western shores of Loch Ness. Although the ride along the loch is really pleasant, apart from the little picturesque village of Drumnadrochit there are few places of note until you arrive at Fort Augustus at the Southern end of the loch. Until the early 18th century it was known as Kiliwhimin, and the Gaelic name for the modern village is still Cill Chuimein. It was renamed 'Fort Augustus' after the unsuccessful Jacobite rising of 1715. It is approached downhill, along a tree lined road with rocky outcrops. When you arrive in the centre it's a lovely little town, nestling in the Great Glen, quite busy with the bustle of holiday makers and it made a pleasant diversion from what had been, until then, a rather quiet even subdued journey.

In the middle of Fort Augustus you go over the old stone road bridge with the river going under, then over the swing bridge where you can see the locks that take the pleasure boats from Loch Ness onto the Caledonian Canal. As you leave the centre you sweep out of the town, having come downhill on entering, as usual, you have to pay by going uphill as you leave. Climbing up out of the town we passed a road sign saying Spean Bridge 23 Fort William 32, as we went past, it entered my mind that with a bit of luck we should be in Fort William in a couple of hours or so.

Keeping on the A82 it then goes through some lovely countryside with isolated cottages, houses and gift shops spread along the route. After a few miles you cross the Aberchalder swing bridge where the Caledonian Canal goes into Loch Oich. Again, you're going along a tree lined road that is nice and sheltered from the wind and you can get an occasional glimpse through the trees of the loch glittering in the morning sunshine.

The road undulates gently and was truly beautiful with all the trees in their summer colour on both sides of the road as it follows Loch Oich going towards Spean Bridge. Where the A87 to The Kyle of Lochalch branches off to the right, we went straight on over the old stone bridge that crosses the Invergarry River. As always from a river, there was an uphill pull out that was a bit sharp and had me breathing heavily but it soon levelled out and before long we were going along the side of Loch Oich and making good progress.

At the end of Loch Oich, we crossed the Laggen swing bridge from where, if you look left, it affords you stunning views up the loch and to the right the Caledonian Canal goes on yet again towards Loch Lochy. We carried on into Glen Albyn following the canal heading for Spean Bridge.

As we rode along, the whole Glen opened up in front of us, on our right were the two massive mountains of Ben Tee 2,957ft and next to it further on Sròn a' Choire Ghairbh at 3,066ft. A mile and a half after the Laggen swing bridge we came to the crest of a short hill, swept round to the left and Loch Lochy came into sight through the trees.

Halfway down the loch we had a magnificent view of the two giant mountains rising straight out of the loch on the far shore, with the trees along the shoreline spreading up the hillside and then thinning out until they disappeared as they got further up the mountains. I called to Bill and pulled over onto a strip of gravel running alongside the road, 'What's the problem?' he called.

'No problem' I replied 'let's have a cigar and just enjoy the view for a minute.' He didn't need asking twice.

We stood there enjoying the beautiful scenery and the cigars, as we looked across the loch. After 10 minutes we were back on our bikes cruising along again. The road followed the shore for about four miles until we reached a small place called Letterfinlay. It then starts to leave the shore and climbs about 380ft in just under a mile which had me gasping for breath and in bottom gear long before we reached the top. From here, the road undulates quite severely but maintaining between 300 and 400ft above sea level for the next four or five miles.

Eventually we came to a small hamlet called Stronaba, right in front of us we could see the giant Aenoch Mor in the distance. I called to Bill, 'Do you see that mountain Bill?'

'Yes' he replied.

'When we get to the foot of that we are as near as damn it in Fort William, halfway for the day.'

As we came out of Stronaba, a vista opened up in front of us and for a few seconds we could see the whole Mamore range spread out in front to the South. Unfortunately, the view soon disappeared as we started to descend from the fell top we had been travelling along. We began picking up speed as we went past the road sign for Spean Bridge and Fort William.

Within seconds we came to a junction where the B8004 forks right off the A82 heading for the A830 for Glenfinnan (where Bonnie Prince Charlie landed before the 1745 uprising) and afterwards it continues on to the beautiful fishing port of Mallaig. I had a quick look behind to check we were clear, put my right arm out and moving into the middle of the road, we turned right up the B8004. I had decided to have a short stop at a well known view point, we turned immediately left onto a car park where a large commemorative granite sculpture of three commandos stands, looking towards the mountains where they had trained during World War Two.

The view of the mountains to the South from here on a nice day, must rank as one of the most outstanding in this country, it is truly magnificent, a word I find totally inadequate to express my real feelings. The whole Mamore range is displayed in a spectacular array stretching from Beinn Chlianaig in the east through Stob Choire Claurigh, Aonach Mor (where the ski slopes are) to Ben Nevis in the west. We got off our bikes, 'Cigar break?' I said to Bill. He didn't answer at first; he just stood there gazing at the mountains for a moment. I had seen the view before but I must admit it never ceases to amaze me, but for Bill this was the first time he had been up this far north.

'That's absolutely incredible,' he said in a quiet voice as he looked out across the valley between us and the mountains.

We walked pushing our bikes up the little slope to the memorial then laid them on the grass and sat down next to them; I took my helmet and gloves off and laid them on the ground. We both lit a cigar and sat there in silence each deep in our own thoughts as we looked along at the incredible view spread out before us.

We were not in a great hurry to move on but when we had finished our cigars I had a quick drink from my bottle and stood up, as I put my helmet back on it was cold to my head where the sweat had gone cold on the sponge padding. 'Come on Bill, it's time we got going.'

'Do you know?' Bill said as he slowly got up and picked up his bike, 'Whatever happens in the next week, whatever struggles we have, it will have been worth it all just to see that view.'

'Yes.' I replied, as I swung my leg over the frame and clipped my cleat in the pedal. 'That is certainly something very special isn't it?'

We set off and cycled back to the A82, as it was still downhill we soon picked up a bit of speed. Just down the road to the left was the large brown sign saying 'Welcome to Spean Bridge', Bill looked across at me and smiled, 'It's been a great run so far today and that view was fantastic' he called.

'Yes' I replied. 'But we are not quite halfway yet and the sting is in the tail today. I can tell you this for nothing; you'll know you've been on a ride by the time you've finished today.'

We sped down the hill really enjoying going through a series of long sweeping bends that we could really motor round. Just as you enter the town the road swings round sharply to the right and you go over the stone bridge across, believe it or not, the River Spean.

The town as you cycle through unfortunately doesn't seem to have a lot going for it on first impressions. It's quite picturesque, nice houses but apart from a Spar, a few bed and breakfast places, a restaurant, The Spean Bridge Hotel and a golf club, that seemed to be it. Oh yes I nearly forgot, there's a Little Chef as you leave on the outskirts of the town. I may be doing the town a disservice as, I must admit, you don't get a lot of time to look around as you cycle through, but that was the impression I was left with.

As always, when you go down to rivers there's more often than not the dubious pleasure of having to go up again when you come out at the other side and Spean Bridge was no exception to the rule. On the road out of town it starts to climb, as you leave the town you pass a sign that says Fort William 10 Crainlarich 62. I called to Bill as we started to drop down the gears, 'Ten miles to lunch Bill, will you make it?'

'Great' he replied, 'it's been a cruise this morning.'

'Yes,' I replied, 'As I said before the only trouble is we still have two of the worst climbs on the trip and the last one ends about 10 miles from Crainlarich.'

We went up the steady climb following the A82; it was a bit of a pull but well worth it as when we got to the top we had good views of the surrounding countryside. It's quite a pleasant road, especially once it levels out and then for most of the way into Fort William it's a long steady descent.

Gathering speed again as we approached Fort William, on our right was a big sprawling white painted building that went under the name of the 'Great Glen Cattle Ranch No 2 Shelter'. Soon after on our left we went past the entrance to the Aenoch Mor Ski area, then as we went passed a little place called Torlundy there's a great cycle track that you can get on that's completely off the road and makes the ride even more pleasant.

Just outside Fort William we came to an Esso filling station on the left so we decided it was time to have our lunch. We pulled into the garage, left the bikes leaning against the front wall and went in, our cleats clattering as we walked across the tiled floor. Having bought ourselves a sandwich, some chocolate and a drink we went out. Picking our bikes up we walked out of the area of the garage and sat at the side of the road on the grass verge watching the traffic go by as we had our lunch.

'Shall we give John a ring and see what's happened?' Bill asked between bites of his sandwich.

'Might as well while we are here, let's hope it's good news.' I said as I reached in my cycling shirt pocket for the phone. I dialled his number and looked at my watch while I waited for him to answer; it was just gone one o'clock. As soon as I heard his cheery voice I relaxed, I could tell it was good news. 'Hi John, how's things with you?' I asked.

'Great, I got the key just after 11 so I'm on my way now. By the time I got back, washed and filled your bottles and hitched up, I got away about 11.45 so I've just gone through Fort Augustus.'

'That's marvellous; we're just having lunch outside Fort William so we should be on our way to Glen Coe when you pass us. If you can find a layby after you've passed us we could do with fresh water bottles.'

'Ok, will do,' came the reply, 'see you soon.' He then hung up.

'Well that's great news.' Bill said after I had repeated what John had told me, 'I can lie back for a moment and enjoy a cigar now' he said, as he finished his lunch and got a cigar out of his shirt pocket.

After half an hour our legs were stiffening up so, as always, it was time to get up, have a stretch and get going again. This time, as we set off I knew we would soon be arriving at the first major climb of the trip: Glen Coe.

The ride through Glen Coe would take us from literally sea level to the summit of Rannoch Moor about 1,148ft. Not excessively steep but constant uphill for about 14 miles and that would be followed with a climb not as high but somewhat steeper perhaps, coming right at the end of the day, the next few hours would be a real test.

As we arrived at Fort William we stuck to the A82 that goes round the town instead of going through the one way system in the centre. It's longer but it's also much more picturesque as it follows the sea wall along Loch Linnhe. As you cycle round you come to a brightly painted white building with an orange roof, built onto a protrusion out into the loch. This is the Crannog Seafood Restaurant, to my mind one of the finest of many very fine seafood restaurants along the west coast of Scotland. It's built on the jetty where the Camusnagaul to Fort William ferry docks.

Leaving Fort William behind, the road follows the shores of the loch for several miles, it's gently undulating and a pleasure to cycle along, apart from the fact that it is narrow and bends a lot in places so occasionally the traffic has to wait to get past you. To your right there are superb views of the mountains rearing up on the other side of the loch. About eight miles from Fort William, just as you reach the turn off for the Corran Ferry, the road leaves the shore for a while.

Just past the ferry turn off, we passed a road sign that told us we were seven miles from Ballachulish and 44 from Crainlarich. 'Won't be long now, only 44 miles, I think I'm finding it a bit easier than the first day.' Bill shouted across as we passed the sign, I must admit I found his optimistic comments quite amusing as he really didn't have a clue what was in front of him, sometimes I thought it would be easier if I didn't as well. But I had to admit the day had been a breeze so far, the ride had been a pleasure and the weather had been great most of the time, although it was changing and becoming more and more cloudy and overcast by the minute.

Just as we were going through Onich, which is quite a rambling village, John passed us with a cheery wave and a toot on the horn, we waved back as he disappeared up the road. I can't explain just how good it was to see that caravan go past.

Then just as we went round a bend yet another memorable sight came into view. As we looked across the waters of Loch Linnie that had also come back into view, there was another amazing array of mountains in front of us. To the right we could see the long ridge going up to the peak of Sgorr Dhearg and then further east just behind but protruding above Meall Mor was the majestic peak of Bidean Nam Bian, the Pride of Argyle as it is known with its satellite Stob Choir Nan Lochan next to it. Finally to our left, Sgorr Na Ciche (The Pap of Glencoe) marking the start of the massive Aonach Eagach ridge.

Within a couple of minutes we were back among trees and the view disappeared but it was obvious that we would soon be starting our first major climb of the trip. As we kept going the mountains began to loom large in the near distance. The next thing we knew, we were crossing Ballachulish Bridge, the bridge that takes you across the loch. We swung over the bridge, the building of which cuts 25 miles off the journey saving you having to go round the loch through Kinlochleven and which, along with the closure of the aluminium smelter which was the major employer in the area, was almost the death of the town.

After the bridge, we went round the roundabout and headed towards Glen Coe, it's about two and a half miles of undulating loch side road to Ballachulish, which we passed on our right without entering the village. Further along the road straight ahead in front of you standing proud is the Pap of Glencoe; this nice little hill is the start of the Aenoch Egach ridge and it is obvious to anyone who sees it where it got its name from. In another mile you enter the village of Glencoe, as you go through the outskirts of the village the road bends to the right, it's from this point that it begins its long, slow, relentless climb into the pass of Glen Coe and up to Rannoch Moor.

About a mile into the glen, just as we passed the Camping and Caravanning Club site, Bill looked at me and pointing up the road said 'Good Lord Fred is there a bl**dy way through that?' I looked up the road to where he was pointing; I knew exactly what he meant as, in the past, I had thought the same. As you look up, the mountains seem to form an impenetrable barrier before you, it just looks as if there is no way through.

'Oh yes,' I replied, 'Oh yes.' I repeated quietly, 'There's a way through alright.'

I was enjoying the beauty of the surrounding mountains as we headed further into the glen, but the climb was beginning to tell and as we passed the tourist centre I was rapidly going down the gears. (The tourist centre is no longer there, following much protesting it was moved to a less conspicuous site lower down the valley by the side of the camping and caravan site.)

It was just then we saw John, pulled up in a layby on the right-hand side of the road, we pedalled up to him and dismounted, laying the bikes on the floor, we walked up to the car. John got out and opened the boot. 'Water gentlemen' he said, we got our (by this time empty) bottles off the bikes, threw them in the boot, got two fresh ones out and slipped them into the cages.

'How's it going so far?' John asked.

'It's been great today' Bill answered, 'But looking up that road in front of us things could be starting to get a little nasty I think.'

John looked up the road, 'Yes it looks quite spectacular doesn't it? Glad I'm going up in the car.' He said smiling.

'You might well bl**dy smile, it's going to be gut busting going up there and if the weather turns bad like it's threatening to, there's nowhere to go' I said, 'still, we're getting there slowly.' After a pleasant 10 minute break we picked the bikes up and took our leave of John and set off up the glen once more.

Further up the road we took the long sweeping left-hand bend onwards and upwards, past the turning on the left which was part of the old road through Glen Coe that leads down to the Clachaig Inn. A great hostelry popular with climbers and walkers, where I have spent many happy hours and sampled some great Scottish hospitality, not to mention quite a few pints as well! This time, however, it was not to be, we had no time to call in, just head down and keep going.

By this time we were really getting into the heart of the glen, the Aenoch Egach ridge loomed up on the left like a massive wall as far as the eye could see. To our right, Aonach Dubh the first of the 'Three Sisters' towered above us with the great slash of Ossian's Cave in its side, and the beautiful Loch Achtriochtan at its foot.

Unfortunately, the weather had taken a turn for the worse and as we got higher we did have a few showers. As it didn't look like doing too much I wasn't too worried about it and just concentrated on pushing those pedals round. Soon I had settled myself into a nice steady rhythm in bottom gear and just kept my legs going at a comfortable pace. I shut my mind to the ache and, as we got higher, the cold as well and concentrated on the ground in front of me. The last time I did this I would get out of the saddle and dig in on occasions then collapse into the seat again, this time I stayed rooted to the saddle.

As we went past the car park on the right near the helicopter landing pad, I began to daydream of the many times I had walked up this road. I recollected the times I had set off across the moors here to cross the River Coe at the 'Meeting of the Three Waters'. From there you can go up through 'The Lost Valley' of Allt Coire Gabhail where it is said the McDonalds took their rustled cattle to hide them. Well I can tell you this, from what I remember about climbing into The Lost Valley I couldn't begin to imagine how they managed to get the cattle up there. Cattle, they must have been more like bl**dy mountain goats.

Allt Coire Gabhail has always seemed to me an amazing place, a place that I never tire of going to. It's quite a hard walk up along a reasonable path but near the top you cross quite a large stream on stepping stones, then you have to cross a great boulder field but once you have got up the steep approach you can look out from above the whole valley. I don't know what it is, but to me standing looking over the valley gives me an eerie feeling. Yet when you drop down onto the valley floor it seems to change to a magical feeling as though this is a special place.

As you carry on along the valley floor heading towards the col that takes you to the Bidien Nan Bian ridge you realise that the river you have followed all the way up the mountain has disappeared, but in the distance you can see a large waterfall in front of you although there is no river or stream coming down the valley. As you get further along towards where the valley starts to curl upward to the ridge you can see the river again in front of you. From a distance it just seems to disappear and you wonder where does it go? It's only as you walk towards it and get almost on top of it that you realise it just disappears into the shingle on the floor of the valley. No matter how often I go there I always find it somehow unreal, just standing there in front of this reasonable size stream that has swept down the mountain, over the waterfall then rushes along towards you just to disappear at your feet and then reappear lower down the mountain.

Anyway, as they say, getting back to the grind, from here the road seems to go a shade steeper and has more twists and turns, which, due to the large numbers of heavy goods vehicles that use this road, makes you feel uncomfortable when you are on a bike. After a while we went through a gap where the road has been cut through the rock and just to the right as you get to the other side is a lovely little waterfall. Just seeing it seemed to lift my spirits which, by this time, were getting a bit low. As I drove myself forever upwards, I concentrated on my rhythm and kept my pedal strokes in beat with my gasping breath. To take my mind off the effort I tried to think of the past and the great times I had had in these mountains walking on sunny days.

Further up the glen you go through another cut out through the rock and finally the valley begins to widen out and loses that overpowering heaviness that has seemed to weigh you down. From here the gradient begins to relent and you can begin to drop a gear or two and start to get your breathing under control. Then just before you arrive at the little hamlet of Altnafeadh, nestled to the right at the foot of the towering Buachaille Etive Mòr, you go over a crest and there is a long stretch of gradual downhill.

As we sped down the slope, the valley opened up in front of us and suddenly cycling became a pleasure again. With the Buachaille and River Coupall on our right and Beinn a' Chrulaiste on our left, the road was leading us towards the middle of Rannoch Moor. In the distance in front of us we could see one of the two, little white steel arch bridges that are on the moor with the famous Kingshouse Hotel further in the distance on our left. The hotel is set among a large group of trees, the only trees as far as the eye could see.

We were bowling along again enjoying the wonderful panorama unfurling in front of us, even though we still had another five miles to go until we reach the summit proper. Once the road started climbing again it was just a matter of dropping a couple of gears and keeping the legs going. As we cycled on up the last 300ft and finally reached the summit of Rannoch Moor, our first major climb of the trip ended as most climbs fortunately do, in an anticlimax. We got to the summit and started the long ride along the plateau before the descent. The view just continued to improve, and the scenery was absolutely stunning as you have the Black Corries to the North, Meall a' Bhuiridh and Stob a' Choire Odhair to the South and all of Rannoch Moor is laid out before you under an immense sky.

As we cycled towards the Bridge of Orchy we were completely surrounded by moor, on the horizon in the distance majestic mountains rose in every direction. If you are ever fortunate enough to go through in good weather it is a place and a view that will live with you for the rest of your life. The road goes on from the summit, undulating for about six miles until we arrived at the small Loch Nan-Achlaise.

On leaving the loch we passed a sign proudly announcing that we were entering Argyll and Bute, soon after we started to descend and before long we were in the highest gear sailing along, enjoying the whole experience. On a left-hand bend where the descent was just changing from gradual to steep, we arrived at a popular viewing point at a layby on the right. Without any hesitation Bill stuck his right hand out and pulled straight on to the layby. 'Let's get a drink and take five.' He said as he dismounted his bike.

'Great, suits me,' I replied. We strolled over to a mobile café van and got a coffee each. As we enjoyed the view over Loch Tulla, and Beinn an Dothaidh we could feel a cold breeze coming across as we were still at a reasonably high altitude.

When I have been through in the past by car and stopped here, there has often been a piper in full national dress waiting for coaches to pull up to unload the tourists. When they get off to enjoy the view, he plays a lament or two, and then waits for the donations. It must be a nice little earner for him in the summer months, but as it happened he wasn't on duty this day.

Walking over to a memorial we laid our bikes on the grass and sat on the floor trying to shelter from the breeze. 'Cigar break?' I said to Bill.

'Too bl**dy true' he replied, 'I thought that last climb was never going to end, I was knackered.'

'Only one more to go' I replied, 'Then it's downhill all the way to Crianlarich.'

Bill lit his cigar and looked at me, 'It can't be as bad as that was surely?' he asked, looking not too chipper. I lit my cigar and leaned back against the memorial enjoying the shelter from the wind as much as the cigar.

'Well, it's not as long that's for sure, but it seems steeper and as you have already done Glen Coe and it's the end of the day, well!' I let my voice trail off leaving him to finish the sentence in his mind.

As we sat and enjoyed our cigars, Bill phoned John; he was well on his way and would be passing us soon. We suggested he carry straight on and find a campsite for the night, set the van up then drive back to pick us up in Crianlarich.

While we sat there I read the memorial, it was dedicated to all the mountaineers who had died in the Scottish mountains and to Hugh T.

Munro who classified all the mountains over 3,000ft and who donated all the land in Glen Coe to the Scottish Nation. The memorial is made of a collection of stones taken from the summit of each 'Munro' i.e. each mountain over 3,000ft.

Eventually, as they say, all good things must come to an end and after finishing our cigars it was time to get on our way again. The first half hour was reasonably exhilarating as we sped down the mountain through the hairpin bends (well nearly hairpin). Although it was not raining it had been not long before and the roads were still wet in places, therefore, it was too dangerous to let yourself go too fast so I kept the brakes applied on the steep parts and good control of the bike on the bends but it was still quite enjoyable.

When we arrived at the bottom I eased up and tried to conserve my energy for the long climb I knew was coming. We cruised along over the second little white arched bridge, the one that when coming in the opposite direction, is always my sign that I have arrived at my favourite place. This time though we were heading south and closing in on the Bridge of Orchy.

Looking north-west from here you can see across Loch Tulla the mountains of Stob Ghabhar and the giant Meall a' Bhuiridh in the direction from which you have come. It was around here that John came cruising past with a low sound of his horn before he got to us and his usual cheery wave as he went past. I don't know why it was but it always gave us a lift when we saw John and the car and throughout the journey the effect would stay the same. It was as if despite the hours of cycling you knew that normality was not far away, or at least what passed for normality on this trip!

The first time I had done this ride on a bike having only done it by car before; I had imagined a long reasonably level run from here through Tyndrum to Crianlarich. I was wrong, soon after passing through the beautiful sounding Bridge of Orchy, which is one of those names that for years had fascinated me and whenever I have been through it, has always seemed as beautifully remote and picturesque as it sounds, it is definitely uphill with a vengeance.

We were now at the bottom of the descent; we passed a sign saying Tyndrum 6 Crainlarich 11, so anyone like Bill who hadn't cycled this way before would be thinking they were almost there. But, unfortunately, the day was not going to give up without that final kick in the teeth for the unwary and the wary alike.

Within a few hundred yards of the sign the road begins to climb. The scenery is still magnificent but now you have left Rannoch Moor behind, the landscape changes. You are now among those mountains that not long ago were just views on the horizon. Tree plantations begin to appear to your right obscuring the view to that side but to the left the mountains rear up alongside you in all their majesty. Having cycled this way before I was confident that I would get up this climb but I knew it wouldn't be easy. I had warned Bill and we had tried to save ourselves some energy, so on the long descent from Rannoch Moor to Bridge of Orchy we had gone at a reasonable pace enjoying the scenery. The first mile after Bridge of Orchy is a slight upward gradient but eventually we arrived at the beginning of the climb proper. The second and third miles are unrelenting; if we thought the climb over the Black Isle was the longest we had ever done after a hard day then this after what had gone before, was worse.

As you cycle up the pass you see the West Highland Railway running alongside you to the left as it contours round the base of the huge cone that is Beinn Dorain. It's the line that goes from Glasgow to Fort William, one I have longed to travel along for as many years as I can remember but as yet have not managed it. As we continued to climb I could hear the breath rasping out of Bill's lungs, my legs started to burn as the lactic acid started to build up. I kept my thoughts focused on my rhythm and my cadence. I was in bottom gear so apart from getting off and walking there was nowhere else to go.

I hit the wall three quarters of the way up and the wonderful scenery suddenly meant nothing. I was fighting to stay on the bike; every turn of the pedals was a nightmare that seemed never ending. My breath sobbed out of me, there was nothing left in my legs, I just knew I had to keep my head down and keep going. However, I was mentally stronger than the first time and managed to just keep my mind concentrating on my rhythm, tying it in with my breathing and just kept pushing those pedals round.

As the climb continued I could see the massive bulk of Beinn Odhar in front of me just to the left, the mighty Beinn Dorain had disappeared over my left shoulder. I knew we were slowly approaching the summit of the pass. But I wasn't going to tell Bill, let the bu**er suffer I thought, this was the way he wanted it, so bl**dy well let him enjoy it. After the third mile the gradient slackened off slightly enabling us to drop a gear and get a brief respite before it kicked up sharply for the last half mile or so.

Gradually we battled our way to the summit, I was ready to carry on as I knew there were two or three miles of fabulous downhill now and then it was just undulating the last few miles into Crainlarich. But at the top Bill pulled off the road near a little gate and stopped exhausted. I pulled off the road onto a gravelled area that led down to the gate.

Bill dropped his bike and gasping said 'For God's sake Fred let's have a cigar, that has absolutely hammered me.' So I got off my bike and leaned it against the gate. Gasping for breath and trying to get my heart rate down I got a cigar out of my pocket, lit up and looked around me. We were on the slopes of Beinn Odhar and behind us was the fabulous cone shape of Beinn Dorain. Alongside us just a few yards away you could see the tracks of the West Highland Railway and just beyond that the well worn path of the West Highland Way.

Bill was sitting on the floor cursing about the climb we had just come up; I must admit after about 10 hours in the saddle and coming after Glen Coe and 100 miles it was a bit of a beast. I sat down on the grass and looked out over the view enjoying my cigar. As soon as I had finished I stubbed it out, took the remains of an energy bar out of my pocket and got my water bottle off the bike. After a bite to eat and a good drink I said to Bill, 'OK mate are you ready to roll?' For the first time since we went through the Berriedale Braes he showed he was suffering. 'Come on,' I said, 'It's a doddle from here on in.' But Bill was in no hurry.

'We'll just have another cigar' he said reaching behind in his jersey for the packet. I could see he wasn't in any mood to set off just yet.

'OK' I replied as I reached for mine. We lit up again and enjoyed another cigar while I lay back on the grass and watched the clouds going past. We must have spent the best part of 30 minutes at the top before Bill got the enthusiasm to get back on his bike again and we set off down the hill.

As we went down we passed the sign that said we were entering the district of Stirling and then just after, another telling us we were entering the Loch Lomond and The Trossachs National Park. We sped down the hill flying along, it's a brilliant downhill stretch where you can really let it go, the bends are long and sweeping and I saw the cycle computer register over 40 miles per hour on the descent.

We flew through Tyndrum, passing the Green Wellie Stop on our left; it's a pleasant enough village an excellent base for touring, camping and walking but not too much there. After about 20 minutes we were entering Crainlarich, ahead of us only a couple of miles away was the huge bulk of the mighty Ben More, 3,822ft of mountain overshadowing the town like some great monster. Finally, after a gruelling day of hard graft, we cycled into Crianlarich and it wasn't a minute too soon, I was shattered.

Just as we passed the turn for Glasgow and went under the railway bridge we spotted John in the car at the side of the road. We pulled up to him; it was just about seven o'clock at night we had been on the road 12 hours. 'How are things?' John enquired.

'Absolutely knackered.' I replied without going into further detail.

'I've got the van set up on a site called Glen Dochart Caravan Park' he replied. 'It's about six miles up the road so if you want to put the bikes in the car I'll get us there'.

We didn't need asking twice, Bill and I took our front wheels off; I got my bike in the boot he got his on the back seat and managed to squeeze in next to it. We both collapsed into the car and set off along the road to the caravan site. 'How has the day been?' asked John. 'We've been through some fabulous scenery.'

'Yes,' I replied 'it was lovely at times on Saturday with the coast and everything but I think this is probably as good as it gets.'

'It was a swine,' came Bill's voice from the back, 'I'm starting to wish I hadn't bl**dy mentioned doing this.' I looked at John and smiled, I didn't say anything but at long last I had a pleasing sense of satisfaction.

It only took a few minutes to get to the campsite which was very nice and quiet. We got Bill's tent up, then he and I went and had a quick shower and got back to the van feeling more our old selves. We emptied and cleaned our bottles ready for the morning and then settled down with a nice drink, coffees all round and three gin and tonics. We had our coffees then went to sit outside with our gin and tonics, Bill and I lit up a cigar each as we enjoyed a much deserved rest. 'I've enquired at the site' says John, 'I believe there is a nice little restaurant within walking distance up the road.'

We walked up the road enjoying the evening air and the feeling of being off the bike. The restaurant was at the Suie Lodge Hotel, it was about half a mile from the site so it was a pleasant stroll. We all had our usual couple of pints then sat down to order our meal.

The meal was excellent and we were soon relaxing with gin and tonics each and Bill and I with our proverbial cigars. The talk was all about the day, we caught up with what John had been doing and how he had picked the key up in Inverness and before we knew it we were on the way home yawning and ready for a good night's sleep.

It had been a nice sunny evening when we left but it was pitch black on the way back, you couldn't see a thing and although there was a torch in the caravan we hadn't thought to take it with us. I must admit the walk back was quite difficult, but for a bit of moonlight it would have been terrible. I sauntered along, drew on my cigar and looked up at the stars, once again wondering at the thousands more that you can see than at home due to the lack of street lights. We eventually got back to the van, Bill got in his tent and John and I got in our sleeping bags. Tonight I was exhausted and really looking forward to getting my head down and getting some sleep.

I lay in my sleeping bag thinking two days gone and approximately 240 miles behind us. I lay rubbing my aching legs thinking about the day. It had been a fabulous day in one respect, but a nightmare in others, yet in general I didn't feel too bad. In my mind, I started to think that I have got over the worst and nothing could be as bad as this. (How wrong can one be?) I felt I was recovering quite quickly and for the first time since the previous John o' Groats to Land's End I have travelled over 100 miles and then done the same the next day. Then I realised it wasn't the next day, we had the break on the Monday. Sod it, I thought, then just as I started to drift to sleep I remembered: I thanked God for delivering us safely through another day, prayed for Chris and then started to think I may just be able to complete this trip with a little luck.

Day's Distance: 115 miles
Cumulative Distance: 238 miles
Day's Climbing: 3,602ft
Total Climbing: 7,322ft

Day 1: John o' Groats camp.

The Old Hotel, John o' Groats, like me, it's seen better days.

Good luck, you'll need it: only 874 miles to go (Bill on the left, Fred on the right).

The toruist's hotel, John o' Groats. The Old Hotel looks more inviting.

The harbour at Helmsdale.

Fairytale Dunrobin Castle, but a dark past.

Foreboding Ruthven barracks.

Into Glen Coe.

This is the life; a wave for John.

The sun doesn't always shine on the righteous.

That camp at Aust.

The last 200 yards. Did you get your chain on or are you freewheeling?

Did you miss me? Chris with Fred at Land's End.

Time for a drink.

The Triumphant Team. Drinks but no cigar. From the left: Fred, John and Bill.

Chapter 7

Day 3 Crianlarich to Moffat

A THREAT TO QUIT, THE BEST CYCLE LANE IN THE WORLD AND THE VIRGIN GETS AN EYEFUL

The third day we got up a bit later after our efforts of the day before, we soon had breakfast and prepared our bottles and got the bikes ready for the ride, Bill had given up on his patent drinks pack on his back after the first day and decided to go back to conventional bottles. Having got ready and taken Bill's tent down, we got our chairs out for five minutes and lit up our first cigars of the day.

I looked across at Bill and said 'Well, shall we make tracks?' He got up slowly off the chair.

'Feeling a bit stiff, but I suppose we should make a move, it's a long day ahead.' He replied as he slowly got up.

'Ok John, we'll get on our way, like we said last night after Glasgow we could get a bit adrift, so if we do get lost you know the route we are planning on taking and if we miss you we'll see you at Moffat.'

John leaned back in his chair and smiled, 'You two have all the fun, but hey, don't worry about me I'll just have to struggle along.'

We left John to break camp, the night before we had suggested putting the bikes onto the car and travelling back to where we got off. However, as it was only five miles or so, we decided to cycle back to where we had finished the day before. There was a reason for this, as where we had stopped the day before, in the centre of Crianlarich you went under the railway bridge, turned left towards Glasgow and you were straight onto a steep climb for a mile or so. So the five mile ride into Crainlarich would serve to get the stiffness out of our legs and get our lungs going before we got to the climb.

The weather was quite miserable as we set off up the road; it was five to eight and today was going to be another long day, approximately 120 miles from Crianlarich to Moffat. Thinking back to the last time I had done it, I thought it was going to be a much easier day than the day before, I couldn't think of any great climbs. We did have to get up to the South Lanarkshire fells, about 500 to 600ft but from what I remembered it was mainly just a long relatively easy climb. Soon enough we had completed the five miles and were turning left after the railway bridge following the sign for Glasgow and we started the climb.

The few miles we had done getting there probably did help our legs a bit but not that much that we noticed. The climb is only about a mile in length but the first section is nearly eight per cent gradient, by the time I had reached the top I'd felt as if I'd used my day's climbing energy in the first quarter of an hour and was back where I finished the night before. Fortunately, the downhill through Glen Falloch is fantastic; it must be about seven miles long, all the way to the northern shores of Loch Lomond and believe me you can really fly, there's no bad bends or anything, it's just head down and go, I loved every minute of the descent.

As you level off you are entering Ardlui and the road isn't quite as pleasant then: it's very picturesque as it meanders along the west bank of Loch Lomond and it is overhanging on both sides with trees but the road is quite narrow and the surface was atrocious. The vibrations were really painful through our hands and arms, the sunlight was constantly affecting us, one minute it was covered by the trees then the next it was in your eyes. Also, wagons were constantly up our backside trying to get past, where there were places to pull in we did to let them get by but these were few and far between. So we cycled like mad listening to the hissing of the pneumatics right behind us as they constantly braked and changed gear trying to get by.

Once we got to Tarbet, however, the road is fine, it's also a dual carriageway in places. All along the west side of the loch, the road is gently undulating and apart from the occasional drop of rain it was a very pleasant ride. The views at times over the loch were spectacular, especially with Ben Lomond in the background on the far side. The A82 along this stretch has a white line about 18in from the verge, this gives you enough room to cycle along a bit like a cycle track and makes you feel slightly separated from the traffic which is somewhat comforting.

About three quarters of the way down the loch you pass a road leading down to a place called Luss, if you are ever up that way it is an enchanting little village right on the shores of the loch, it is a conservation area and is almost exactly as it was over 100 years ago.

The morning had gone really well, we had by now, left Loch Lomond behind and were rapidly reducing the miles to Glasgow when suddenly my mind went back to the Sunday when we arrived on the outskirts of Inverness. Bill's reaction when he had seen Kessock Bridge had caught me by surprise, I never realised he had vertigo until that moment. Now the words I had shouted in disbelief when he told me he had vertigo struck me out of the blue. I vividly remembered saying, 'If you don't like this, wait until you see the Erskine Bridge.' I suddenly realised that the event which I had blurted out to him at the time was rapidly approaching. We were about 10 miles from the bridge and soon we would be able to see it in all its impressive glory and suddenly I wasn't feeling confident of his reaction when he saw it.

We cycled along with Bill in the lead, I waited for what I knew was the inevitable, I didn't have to wait long and the reaction was, if anything, worse than I had expected. We were going along the Dumbarton Road, going uphill slightly, just before it changes to the Great Western Road when I saw it, just in front to the right in the distance. At that same moment I realised Bill had seen it too, he jammed the brakes on that quickly I nearly ran into the back of him. 'Bl**dy hell Bill, what's the matter?' I asked, pretending I hadn't realised what he had seen. 'I nearly ran in the back of you.'

'Don't bl**dy tell me what that is' he shouted pointing across to the bridge in the distance and then repeating himself just in case I hadn't heard the first time.

'Right, I won't,' I said, 'let's get a move on we haven't got all day to stand about chatting.' But Bill wasn't going to be side tracked so easily.

'If you think for one minute you're getting me over that bl**dy monstrosity you can go and plait bl**dy cabbage.' I looked at him and quickly realised I wasn't going to get anywhere talking to him, so thinking quickly I said 'Look Bill, there's a layby up the road we'll get to that, have a cigar and think what we can do.'

We set off up the road after about 10 minutes we pulled into the layby about one or two miles from the bridge. 'I'm not going over that bl**dy bridge' Bill said with determination in his voice 'there's no bl**dy way you're going to get me over that thing.'

'Look Bill' I said, 'We have to go over.'

'What do you mean *have to*, is there no other way round?' he shouted.

'Well there must be a way somewhere through Glasgow but I don't know the way and it could take us hours.'

In all honesty I must admit I felt sorry for him, he looked dreadful but we were committed and I knew we had to get across that bridge. 'Right' he says, 'Phone John, I'll wait here and flag him down then I'll get in the car and put the bike in the van.' I looked at him and realised he wasn't joking.

'Look Bill you can't cycle from John o' Groats to Land's End and do part of it by car, you'll ruin everything you've worked for all these months.' He looked straight at me.

'I don't care' he says, 'Just get him to stop and pick us up.'

I thought quickly, what could I do? I decided I had two options. One was to get him over that bridge, the other was to go through Glasgow with him. I made my mind up, it would have to be one of those two, I was sure Bill would never forgive me if I let him get in the car and go over the bridge. He may have been happy to do that now, but I felt sure that afterwards if we finished our ride he would have been disappointed not to have cycled the whole route.

'OK,' I said. 'I'll give him a ring.' I took the phone out of my pocket and dialled John. His cheery voice soon came down the earpiece. 'Look John where are you?' I asked, as I ever so slowly walked away from Bill one step at a time.

'Just a couple of miles from the Erskine Bridge,' came his reply.

I kept slowly edging away from Bill. 'Look,' I said, 'we are in a layby just in front of you; it's just after a roundabout.'

'I see a roundabout sign up the road in front of me' he answered.

I dropped my voice 'Look John' I whispered, 'We've got a slight problem but whatever you do don't stop, do you hear me?' John must have wondered what was going on.

'Are you sure, what's the matter?'

'Yes' I replied, 'I'll tell you later but whatever you do don't stop, OK.'

'Right I don't understand but I've got you, see you soon.' He replied as he hung up.

I put the phone back in my pocket and walked back to where Bill stood. 'He's only a couple of minutes away, might as well have a cigar while we wait,' I said getting a cigar out of the packet.

'Great,' said Bill getting one of his cigars out. Just as we lit them we saw John coming up the hill, Bill rushed down the layby waving to him as if to pull him in, John gave a wave back and sounded the horn as he carried on up the road.

Bill's face was a picture, for a brief moment I really felt sorry for him, well almost. Right Bill, I thought this was your bl**dy idea and now by God you're bl**dy going to carry on with it, rough with the smooth. He turned to me as if pleading, 'He didn't stop! He didn't stop! What can we do?' he cried. I took a long pull on my cigar and looked at him.

'We can get on our bikes and get over that damn bridge' I said, in a determined voice. He looked at me and I could tell by his face that he had got a grip of himself.

'OK' he said, 'Finish this cigar and we'll get going.'

The approach to the bridge normally is a bit dicey; as we cycled towards it there was a road which joins it from the left to make a dual carriageway. This means you have to get across this other road to get on the inside and as it is a national limit road the traffic is coming through pretty damn quick.

As we cycled round we could now see the bridge rearing up in front of us and just down the road was a temporary 30mph speed limit sign. All along us to the left were cones tapering from the inside lane to make the traffic join ours. By pure good luck it turned out they were carrying out works to the bridge and fortunately, or unfortunately whichever way you look at it, the cycle lane along the edge of the bridge and the first traffic lane were shut off.

This meant, of course, we were cycling alongside all the cars and juggernauts in a quite narrow lane. However, it also meant we weren't on the cycle lane on the edge of the bridge with the fantastic panorama and the horrendous drop in full view. 'Look,' I shouted to him as we started up the rise towards the bridge. 'Remember Inverness, stick close behind me and don't look to the side, keep your eyes on my wheel.'

'I've no bl**dy intention of looking over the side, do you think I'm mental or something?' He shouted across to me, leaving me in no doubt that he wouldn't be tempted to have a quick glimpse.

I glanced behind, Bill looked almost cheery; I thought to myself, God that was a stroke of luck, these road works pushing us into the middle of the bridge, it just goes to show the devil looks after his own. I soon had something to take my mind off Bill as due to the curve of the bridge and the exposure to the elements it made the crossing quite arduous though thankfully reasonably short. At the other side as we came off the bridge and saw the signs for the motorway in front of us, we immediately turned left onto the A898 sign posted Bishopton and Erskine. We went down a long sloping slip road to the roundabout turned right on the A726 and started heading across country.

Bill had soon recovered from his ordeal and as we skirted round Glasgow airport heading for Paisley he was back to his bubbly self. We were heading for East Kilbride and Strathaven, all on the A726 and then making our way to the B7078.

From here as far as East Kilbride, approximately 20 miles, it would be built up areas all the way so our rhythm and average speed would suffer as we were forever having to stop at traffic lights, road junctions and the like. It's also slowly but constantly increasing in height as you get further east.

After what seemed an inordinate length of time we finally rode out of the built up areas, as we swung round a roundabout on the A726 following the Strathaven signs we were finally heading out into the countryside again. For the next six miles or so it was really pleasant with outstanding views out to the west until we came into Strathaven.

Leaving the roundabout the road went steeply up in front of us; we noticed a cycle track over on the right-hand side of the road so we swung over and got on the track. 'Hang on' Bill called, 'Let's have a cigar break.' So seeing the slope on the road ahead I swung off the bike and laid it on the grass verge.

'We may as well have a bite to eat while we are stopped.' I answered, getting an energy bar out of my pocket.

We sat on the grass enjoying the break; after I'd eaten I had a drink from my energy drink bottle then from my water bottle to freshen my mouth. After putting them back on the bike I got out a cigar, lit it and lay back on the grass enjoying the feeling of the smoke and resting of my aching body. After a changeable start to the day the sun had come out and it was now quite pleasant, I started to drift off thinking about Chris and the kids, wondering what they were doing and if they ever thought about where I was and what I was doing. After 10 minutes that seemed to pass like two, it was time to be off again up the steep hill. After a day of reasonable riding this was a rude awakening, not remembering any bad climbs on this stretch it was hard to feel your legs going and gasping for breath as you slowly crawled up the hill with your front wheel wobbling. We dug in and soon the road levelled off a bit, after another few miles we entered Kirkmuirhill.

We went under the M74 and straight through the village, after about a mile we hit the B7078 and turned right heading towards Moffat. After the climb from the Clyde valley even though it had been a gradual climb in the main, it was good to find yourself 'on the top' so to speak and cruising along at a nice pace across undulating countryside.

The B7078 must be the best 'B' road in the country, certainly along this stretch, as after the first couple of miles it becomes a four lane dual carriageway for quite a distance. I think it used to be the old A74 and now they had opened the M74 there was hardly anything on it. We carried on for several miles until we reached a large double roundabout that took us under the motorway. This took us past the Happenden services, the ones after Abington where we had stopped on the way up.

As we carried on past the services we went back under the motorway, this side was just two lanes but the white line on the edge of the road was about three foot from the verge so we cycled casually along this space without a care in the world. This stretch along the B7078 (Carlisle Road) was without doubt the most pleasant period of cycling during the whole trip. There was hardly anything on the road, there were several climbs but nothing to slow you much and you could see for miles over open country, it was a joy to cycle along.

A mile or so after the services at Happenden you go up a long reasonably steep climb then as you get to the top you suddenly come across a brilliant cycle lane; it's where the road used to be a four lane dual carriageway before they opened the motorway. Now they have made the road into a two lane carriageway, then they had dug up one lane of the other carriageway and left the far one as a cycle track. It must be one of the best cycle lanes in the world. Unfortunately, while we were on it there was hardly as much as a car came along in either direction on the main road so despite having a wonderful cycle track it was a bit wasted.

Approximately 10 miles after the Happenden services you arrive at Abington, we didn't stop to relive our earlier visit when we were travelling up, we just carried on legs whirling round keeping a nice tempo going. From here the road changes to the A702 and you stay on it until it takes a sharp right under the motorway sign posted Glasgow. Here we carried straight on staying on the same side of the motorway on what had now become the B7076 sign posted Beattock and, of all places, Carlisle. Bill gave a whoop of joy, 'We're heading for good old England' he cried.

'We have been for the last three days,' I replied. 'The trouble is we still have another three and a half days to go once we get there.'

The remainder of the day passed without incident and quite pleasantly, apart from one light-hearted moment. We were just cycling along enjoying the scenery about an hour and a half from Moffat, most of the route had been quiet since we had got onto the B7078 and 7076 but we had just got to a really quiet spot away from the motorway when Bill asked 'did I fancy stopping for a cigar break?' I agreed, so we got off the bikes, laid them on the grass, sat down beside them and got our cigars out.

We were sitting there miles away from any kind of civilization, enjoying the sunshine and listening to the birds when Bill decides he needs to attend to a call of nature. The road being totally quiet I said, 'Just pop down behind that shrub.' But no, Bill decides to get right off the road and goes down the slope so as not to be seen by any passing car. Before Bill gets down to the job in hand he has to take his cycling top off to get his bib shorts down so to all intents and purposes he's virtually naked. So there he is squat down, staring up the embankment not a care in the world, pondering the mystery of the universe and enjoying the quiet pleasures of life with his backside stuck out in the air behind, when all at once the Virgin Inter City express comes thundering past about 25 yards behind him. I thought it was hilarious, Bill somehow, at the time, didn't see the funny side of it. No doubt a few dozen passengers got more of the Scottish scenery than they expected that day.

After Bill had sorted himself out and scrambled up the slope looking quite abashed, we set off on the final lap to Moffat. The last hour of the day passed quite pleasantly, bowling along this great road following the A74M. The last 10 miles being downhill, we set a good pace and were entering the outskirts of Moffat about quarter past seven.

Moffat is a pleasant little village where I have stayed many times as a break on my way to and from the Highlands. We had always planned to stay at the Camping & Caravan Club site there. Arriving at the site about 7.30 we cycled round until we found the car and van. John greeted us warmly; we hadn't seen much of him that day so it had been a long lonely old day for him.

We got Bill's tent up, then rapidly had our showers and got changed. It was a lovely night so we got the chairs out and after the customary feet up with a cigar and gin and tonic, we strolled leisurely up to the village. When in Moffat we usually eat at the Black Bull, for two reasons really, one, it's the nearest and two the food is always reliable, so that's where we dined this night.

We each ordered a pint while we looked at the menu, I remember thinking, I need some carbohydrate to replenish the energy stores, so I ordered macaroni cheese. I can't remember what starter I had but I know I shouldn't have had it as I could only manage to eat half my main course.

We ordered another pint to have with our meal and after the meal a gin and tonic each. While Bill and I enjoyed a cigar, we sat relaxing feeling full and enjoying the tired feeling after a hard day well done. We filled John in on our adventures during the day, he in his turn gave us the low down on what he had been up to and we discussed how we were bearing up in general after two consecutive days on the road.

After a well deserved and enjoyable meal we strolled back to the campsite; again, you could see thousands of stars and make out the Milky Way stretching across the night sky. We got back to the van and sat outside with another gin and tonic each. Bill and I sat back enjoying the last cigars of the day while we discussed with John the plans for the next day.

I had decided in my own mind to make it a big day mileage wise if we could, with us losing a day I knew it was going to be a struggle to meet up with Chris and our friends who were going to a lot of trouble and expense to see us arrive at Land's End.

I mentioned getting to Wigan, or Preston at least if Wigan wasn't possible, the consensus was that it wasn't possible. The truth was, I knew that as well as them, I was just desperate to get to Land's End early Monday evening. Anyway we decided to leave fixing the stop until the last moment tomorrow to give us a chance of getting as far as possible without taking too much out of us. The only saving grace was that the following two days after tomorrow would be relatively easy after what we had been through so far and what was to come tomorrow.

Settling down in the sleeping bag I was feeling quite good, exhausted but good. My legs were aching, in fact I was aching all over but we had got over three of perhaps the worst days of the trip and had covered 350 miles. Plus, we had finally done well in excess of 100 miles two days on the run. As always, I thought of Chris and our kids then I started to pray to give thanks to God who had brought me so far safely, but before I had finished I was asleep.

Day's Distance: 113 miles
Cumulative Distance: 351 miles
Day's Climbing: 2,474ft
Total Climbing: 9,796ft

Chapter 8

Day 4 Moffat to Beetham
DETOURS, RAIN, SHAP AND A RABBIT

Before I knew where I was, the alarm was going off, I went to leap out of bed but it didn't happen, there was no leap in me. I looked across the van to where John was just stirring. 'Gordon Bennett!' I cried 'I feel knackered this morning.' I fully unzipped my sleeping bag to let me get my legs out. Putting my feet and legs over the side I slowly got myself sat up on the edge of the settee. Looking around I tried to get some life into me. 'Feeling a bit stiff and achy this morning John.' I said as I got to my feet, I slowly bent down and touched my toes to stretch my hamstrings.

'Probably the alcohol from last night' he said in a cheery manner.

'That's all I want,' I gasped as I fell back on the settee rubbing my legs, 'With today being hopefully a long one and certainly worse than yesterday.'

I knew if we could do what I hoped, today would be the furthest we would travel and we had to go over the Shap, not something I was looking forward to. The first section of the ride down to the end of the A74M was through quite lovely scenery; unfortunately this was followed by one of the scariest sections of the whole route. The six to seven miles between the A74M and the M6 is a four lane dual carriageway and the juggernauts come straight off the one motorway and carry on at 60 to 70 miles per hour heading for the M6. I can tell you when these trucks come past you within three feet, at that speed you feel the suction from them, it's frightening.

Fortunately they have completed the motorway now so the M6 now goes onto the A74M without a break and so it must be much safer these days. Anyway the night previously we had decided to avoid this stretch by turning left on the A6071 to Longtown then south again on the A7 towards Carlisle where you then get on the A6. It would be a bit further but in the scale of things it would be negligible and we hoped it would be safer and a bit more enjoyable.

Before long we had had breakfast, taken Bill's tent down and were ready to go or as ready as we would ever be that day. It was 7.15am when we cycled out from the site and along the mile or so that led back to the A74M. Going round the roundabout we continued on the A701 past Beattock and then got onto the B7076. This little road was going to follow the motorway and accompany us all the way to Gretna Green.

It's a great part of the ride this as you go through some very pleasant scenery on a reasonably quiet road that takes you through the towns of Johnstonebridge, Lockerbie and a place I always think should be in Wales when I see the sign, Ecclefechan. It's also one of those roads where you can keep up a good average speed as, apart from a couple of small rises, it's just undulating downhill all the way to Gretna Green.

Before we knew it, we were entering the outskirts of Gretna, we pulled up next to a large boarded up hotel and lit a cigar each. 'Did I ever tell you about the time I cycled over the Erskine Bridge?' Bill asked with a smile on his face.

'No' I answered 'But I can tell you this, you weren't bl**dy smiling like that when you knew you had to go over it.' We stood in the morning sunshine enjoying our cigars. As soon as we had finished I got us on our way again as I knew we didn't have time to hang about.

We set off and took the diversion we had planned, compared to the last time I had done it when we stayed on what was then the A74 it seemed to take ages but at least I didn't feel I was playing Russian roulette with the juggernauts. Although there were still a lot of heavy goods vehicles along the route we took, at least they weren't doing 60 or 70 miles an hour as they went past.

The approach to Carlisle from the north is through a built up mixture of residential and commercial properties. We cycled into the centre of Carlisle which I always think is quite an attractive town and a place I would like to go and stay for the weekend but we couldn't hang about today, we were just passing through. We soon picked up the A6, a road that we were going to stay with all day and some of the following day as well. Most people, when you mention the A6 think of built up industrial conurbations. Especially those who live near me where the A6 goes through Stockport and Hazel Grove and in a car it can take you half a hour to go a couple of miles but south of Carlisle you have mile after mile of gentle rolling countryside all the way to Penrith.

It's 18 miles from Carlisle to Penrith, a small town with a one way system through the centre, we had done about 63 miles since we had set off. Most of the last 20 miles had been gradually uphill, the last few miles into Penrith, however, had been downhill but after this it was going to be mainly hard uphill for the next 15 so we decided to get a bite to eat.

Soon we came to a pedestrianised area, so we got off our bikes and walked along, our cleats clattering on the floor, until we came to a shop with tables outside that sold hot pies and hot drinks. We both decided on a meat and potato pie and pot of coffee, we then settled at one of the tables outside, leaning our bikes against the shop wall. The weather wasn't looking great at this time; in fact, it was looking grim and a bit chilly so we were the only ones sitting outside.

After having a nice bite to eat, a hot drink and the proverbial cigar it was time to get on our way. We got back on the bikes and set off, finding the A6 we were soon out of town, within minutes we were back out into the country again. This stretch of the A6 is a great road for cycling along: reasonably comfortable cycling going through nice countryside but it was always, imperceptibly at first but then more noticeably, rising.

As we got slowly higher and the road started ever so slowly getting steeper the weather began to close in. The clouds got lower and darker, 'It looks like we are in for a bit of bad weather' Bill said as we cruised along slowly dropping through the gears. I was breathing heavily by this time, as for quite a while it had been a constant gradient, not too steep but just a bit too steep for comfort.

About 11 miles from Penrith we entered the village of Shap, just then it started to rain, the gradient relented somewhat as we enter the village and for a mile or two it lulls you into a false sense of security. But it soon picked up again as once more we started a relentless climb, not steep but one that goes on and on for a couple of miles or so.

Then all at once it went downhill and you think great, as your legs fly round and the wind rushes past you. But don't be fooled, this is a brief respite and within a mile the road starts to curve upward again and every inch you enjoyed going down has to be fought back up again. Shap village was to be the last piece of proper civilisation we came to until we got over the summit of the Shap and down the other side into the outlying areas of Kendal.

The road slackened off slightly but kept climbing, gradually at first but getting steeper the further we got up, the rain was coming down and as we got higher the wind seemed to be getting up. We went past a conifer plantation to the left of us but unfortunately the wind was coming from the right so there was no respite from its relentless battering. We continued to climb, the countryside was barren now and the weather got wilder. By this time I had been struggling in bottom gear for quite some time; the road got steeper still as we came up along a rocky outcrop on our left forming a low cliff. How I wished it had been on our right to give us some protection from the wind.

I was really fighting the elements as well as the ponderous pull of gravity on my 13 stone and rapidly weakening frame. The wind felt like a gale as I dug in, breath coming in gasps, as we went higher the wind seemed to hit you from the right then bounce of the cliff face and buffet you again. By this time I was riding on instinct, I had shut off to outside influences; I didn't even notice the juggernauts passing too close at times. I lived in my mind, my breathing went with my pedal rhythm, my chest was thumping like a drum. It seemed as if I could hear it above the howling of the wind; I wondered if my heart was going to give out, but by now I didn't care, death would have been a release from the constant torture of pushing myself up this mountain.

The rain kept driving down, the wind blew harder, my gasping breath was now as loud as the wind; I rode on and on in a trance until finally without noticing at first, the gradient began to slacken. Very slowly my gasping started to diminish and my heart began to come under control again.

I realised that the road had swung round to the left and the wind had now started to blow from an angle slightly behind us, then another conifer plantation appeared but to our right this time giving us a bit more shelter. So, this along with the slackening of the gradient, is what had resulted in me getting my breath back and lowering my heart rate.

I came out of the trance I had been in and started to look about, I noticed the rain was slackening off, but by this time we were wet through anyhow. I did a quick check of my physical condition, though we were still going uphill the gradient was negligible now but I felt absolutely goosed. The cumulative effect of the last two days added to the last half hour had left me totally drained.

I knew we weren't far from the summit and from there it was several miles downhill to Kendal that would give me some time to recover so I was beginning to feel better when I noticed Bill a way in front of me. The road was very quiet just then; there was no traffic about so I started to catch him up, when all at once a small rabbit ran out from the side of the road near Bill who had to swerve to miss it. Having avoided Bill it then saw me, turned away and started to hop back up the road.

Whether it was ill or just too young I don't know but it didn't go dashing off like they usually do; in fact, it started zigzagging just in front of me. I did all sorts to escape it, I slowed down, sped up, swerved to the left then to the right, everything possible. I almost fell off the bl**dy bike trying to avoid it. Then right at the last second it darted across in front of me and I saw it go under the front wheel and felt the bump, bump as I went over it with both wheels.

Horrified I looked back as I carried on cycling, there was no way I was going to stop, I'd never have got going again if I had. I was bl**dy annoyed after everything I had done to miss the damn thing but there it was just getting to its feet and staggering down the road. I don't know if it died after but I wouldn't think for one minute that a guy over 13 stone and a bike going over it on 25 millimetre tyres would have done it a whole lot of good.

I caught up to Bill just before we arrived at the summit, 'Bl**dy hell! Fred, I couldn't do that again, I hope it's the last hill we have to go up.' He gasped at me.

I looked at him and smiled 'Bill, what have I told you?' I shouted across, 'There's always another hill.' He looked at me as if he was going to burst into tears, 'But you're OK it's downhill virtually the rest of the way today.' I replied. Then just as I finished speaking I looked up and wonder of wonders, there in the distance we saw the caravan in a layby just by the summit.

You could not imagine the relief and joy I felt as I saw the van. 'Thank God for John' I shouted as we made our way across, 'that's what I call a sight for sore eyes if ever I saw one' I exclaimed. John got out of the car when he saw us coming and opened the van door.

'Fancy a drink?' he asked as we got off the bikes and leaned them against the van.

'That sounds fantastic' Bill said as he climbed into the van.

I climbed into the van, got two towels out and threw one to Bill, 'Here get yourself dry while we wait for the kettle to boil and we can get changed out of these wet things.' We got dried, stripped off and into fresh cycling gear. 'I feel a million times better already, fancy a cigar Bill?'

'Just the job.' He looked much brighter as well now as he sat down on the settee at the front of the van. We pulled out the cigars, the packets were a bit soggy but the cigars were fine in their individual cellophane wrappings.

John passed us our coffees, 'I'll leave the gas ring on to warm the van up a bit,' he said.

'Great,' I replied as I took a long drag on my cigar. 'Good grief that feels better than anything I could think of, you can't imagine what it's been like coming up that bl**dy hill' I gasped as I took a sip of my coffee.

'It didn't look good' John replied 'It buffeted the caravan about a bit as I was coming up, so I thought you may need a break when you got to the top.'

It's surprising what getting dry, a nice warm change of clothes, a hot drink and a cigar can do for you. After 20 minutes we had gone from death's door to being ready and raring to go. 'It's a good easy ride for the next hour or so' I said, 'We can fly downhill to Kendal even if the road is wet there are no bad turns going down there. Then it's just a bit tricky getting in the right lanes to go through the one way system in Kendal' I said to Bill.

By the time we had finished our drinks and cigars we were stiffening up so it was time to get out there again. We said our goodbyes to John and set off down the A6, this time going into the valley leaving the worst of the elements behind us.

From leaving the van we were approximately 12 miles from Kendal, the run down into the town is exhilarating as you can really get up some speed, it's not too steep and there are some really long straights and, as I said, no bad bends so it was head down and go for it. The countryside as you get down from the high top becomes gentler, nice farmland on either side of the road. This is what I think cycling is all about, going downhill flying along with no effort about 35, 40 miles an hour. Unfortunately, much quicker than we went up the other side, we were soon at the bottom and entering Kendal.

It was about six o'clock in the evening when we entered Kendal so it was quite busy but we managed to negotiate the one way system and get into the correct lanes without any trouble. We headed out of town on the A6 until we hit the A591 which is the main dual carriageway that takes you into the Lake District heading for Windermere and Ambleside, a very busy and fast road. However, there is a cycle track along the length of it up to the next junction where you join the A590 before heading down the A6 again leading to Milnthorpe.

As we got on the A6 just before we entered Milnthorpe, we phoned John to see what the situation was, he had passed us before we got through Kendal. As it was getting late he had gone on up the A6 and sited the van about 20 miles up the road. It had been decided that today we would go to our own homes and would all sleep there to give us a break, refresh us and get some cycling gear washed. Unfortunately we had fallen drastically behind schedule due to one reason or another. As I said, by tonight I had been hoping to be through Preston, as it was we hadn't even got to Lancaster and were still 36 miles from Preston, it was seven o'clock and we decided we had to call it a day.

When we spoke to John he had already realised we weren't going to get much further so he had sited the caravan on a Caravan Club certified location at Olde Duncombe House which was opposite the Roebuck Inn at Billsborough. It was agreed that we would keep cycling down the A6 and he would drive up and pick us up wherever he met us.

As it happened he arrived in the car just as we got to Beetham, he pulled up in a layby and we got off the bikes and took the wheels off to get them in the car, again I was in comfort in the front and Bill was snuggled up next to his bike in the back.

As we pulled onto the caravan site John explained that he had booked in at the Premier Lodge which was just across from the caravan site. 'I phoned Christine and she is on her way up with my change of gear so we are both staying there for the night.'

'That's a great idea,' I replied as we got out of the car and took the bikes out, we put the wheels on and left them in the van. 'It will save me dropping you off at home and give me a bit more time as well.'

So Bill and I packed our dirty cycling gear, said our cheerio's to John and got in the car, as we drove down the A6 I lit a cigar and opened the window. 'Well Bill, it's not gone as well as I had planned; by the time we get home it will be getting quite late.'

Bill lit his cigar and agreed, 'Look Fred, I'll phone Gill and she can pick me up at the Bolton services where she dropped me off. It will save you a lot of time.'

I readily agreed, so he got his mobile out and was on to Gill straight away. By the time we arrived at the services she was waiting for him. We got out of the car, I opened the boot and he reached in and got his bag out. 'Plenty clothes for you to get washed and dried tonight' I said to Gill.

'He may have to do them himself,' she replied smiling. 'Look, tomorrow instead of you picking him up here, I will take him back to the caravan, what time are you meeting?' she asked.

'Having a late start tomorrow so we are meeting at eight o'clock' I replied.

'OK we'll see you then, have a good night, what's left of it by the time you get home.' She called.

I got back in the car and waved to them as I set off down the M61. I lit another cigar and settled back in my seat getting comfortable. It must have been about 9.30 in the evening when I pulled on the drive at home. I got out and grabbed my gear out of the boot, taking my key out, I opened the door and walked in.

'Anyone at home?' I called as I walked up the hall towards the living room. Chris was already coming out; I dropped the bag as she came towards me and put her arms around me. I gave her a kiss and a big hug, 'I've brought you a present,' I said looking down at the bag.

'Thanks' she said, 'I can imagine what it is, how are you darling? You're late.' she said as she bent down and picked up the bag.

'Fine' I replied, 'Aching all over, but fine.'

'Steak, chips, peas, tomatoes and mushrooms as you requested. Do you want to open a bottle of wine?' She asked. I went into the dining room and walked over to the wine rack, looking through the reds I chose a bottle of Crozes Hermatage and walked into the kitchen to get the bottle opener. I remember thinking, God it's good to be back home, I couldn't care if tomorrow never came and it wouldn't bother me if I never got on that bl**dy bike again.

I took the cork out of the bottle and smelled the aroma, I could smell the meal from the dining room it was heaven. I poured myself and Chris a glass, put the bottle on the dining table and then went to sit in the living room. I put Chris's glass on the coffee table, put my feet up on the settee and switched the telly on. News at Ten came on; I sat enjoying my drink and watching it quite avidly for a few minutes. I suddenly realised that for almost a week we had been totally involved in our own little world, not seeing any news programme or even a newspaper if it came to that. We knew nothing: only pedalling, the road, the route and suffering.

Chris called me from the dining room, 'Dinner's up', I got up, turned the television off and picked up her glass of wine. I walked into the dining room and sat down in my usual place facing the window. Chris brought the dinner in and sat down along the side facing the fireplace. It looked and smelt great; I put loads of pepper and vinegar on the chips and a pile of English mustard on the side of my plate.

As we ate Chris chatted about how our ride was going and asked what seemed a never ending stream of questions and then eventually she came to the main one. Did we think we would get to Land's End for the Sunday or would it be Monday? I explained that at first I had hoped we would get there by Sunday but as we had failed to make up any time, in fact we had lost time today, so I couldn't see us getting there for Sunday but I hoped to get there for a reasonable time on Monday. 'Well we've booked the bed and breakfast now, so we will just have to go down and hope for the best. Sandy and I have to be back at work on Tuesday morning.' She said in a resigned tone.

I locked up and went upstairs to bed while Chris was sorting the washing; I set the alarm for 6am, got in the shower and gave myself a good wash. I stood there for a few minutes enjoying the hot water running over my aching body. I shut my eyes and could have drifted off to sleep; I shook my head to wake myself up a bit then stepped out. I dried myself and walked over and got in the bed next to Chris. We automatically put our arms round each other and kissed, 'I love you more than I can say' I said. I just about heard her reply as I fell asleep, the next moment the alarm was going off.

Day's Distance: 100 miles
Cumulative Distance: 451 miles
Day's Climbing: 2,369ft
Total Climbing: 12,165ft

Chapter 9

Day 5 Beetham to Whitchurch
THE CROWDS COME OUT TO WAVE, SHORT CUTS AND A FIRST PUNCTURE

The alarm went off, as I woke up for a moment I was totally confused, I couldn't remember where I was but then it flooded back to me. I lay there with my eyes shut thinking of what lay in store, I would have given anything, all the money in the world to turn over, go back to sleep and never ever get on that bike again. I struggled up and sat on the edge of the bed with my head in my hands.

'You OK?' Chris's voice came to me.

'Yes, great,' I lied, 'I'll just have a quick shower to wake me up, you stay in bed.' I got up, went to the bathroom, cleaned my teeth and got under the shower. By the time I'd dried myself, dressed and gone downstairs, Chris had put her dressing gown on, gone down and got my clothes out of the dryer.

I had a quick breakfast of two pieces of toast and took another two with me to eat when I arrived at the caravan before we set off. I collected everything together, picked up my car keys and unlocked the door. Chris stood there with my cycling gear in the bag; I took hold of her and felt her warm and soft next to me, I kissed her. 'I'll miss you.' I said.

'I'll miss you too but you're over halfway now, it won't be long till we see you on Monday, keep yourself safe.' I walked out and opening the car door threw my things in the back.

'Say a prayer for me each day' I said, as I got in and turned the ignition on.

'I will' she said and as she waved to me I drove off.

As I went down the road my heart felt heavy until I got going, I lit myself a cigar and turned the radio on, I couldn't be bothered with the Talk Sport or Radio Four so I settled for Classic FM. I relaxed as I drove up the M60 and M61 heading north for the M6. The traffic was still pretty light as I started heading up past Preston and on towards Lancaster. I lit another cigar and thought about the day ahead; looking at the clock on the dashboard it showed 7.30. Today and tomorrow were going to be two of the easiest days of the trip, so I ran through my mind the places we would be going through. As I have spent most of my working life in the North West I knew the route pretty well and I knew there were no horrors waiting for us today but the traffic would be the worst we had encountered.

Coming off the motorway at junction 33, I was soon on the A6 heading up to the caravan site. I arrived just about eight o'clock as we had arranged, John and Christine were already there having just come across the road from the hotel. As I pulled up and got out of the car John was unlocking the van door.

'Looking forward to getting going again?' he asked brightly.

'Can't wait,' I replied trying to put a bit of enthusiasm in my voice, 'I've been thinking about it on the way up, today's going to be an easy run it's downhill all the way to the Cheshire plain.'

'There's a good climb up out of Warrington.' John said.

I pulled my face and answered, 'Yes but after what we've been through it's only a small hill.'

'Did you have a good night?' Christine asked, as I got my bag out of the car and headed towards the van.

'Yes it was great, a nice change, a bit short mind you after the travelling to get there, how was your hotel?'

'Oh it was quite comfortable, good value.'

Just as I finished speaking Bill and Gill pulled onto the site, I went in the van and started to get changed. John had already put the kettle on. 'Thought you may want a brew before you set off,' he said.

'That's a great idea; I have some toast here so I'll have a bite as well before we get going.' After a couple of minutes I had my cycling gear on and went outside to see Gill before she left. 'Hi love, how are you?' I asked.

'Feeling good, we had a nice meal and a quiet couple of hours before we went to bed, just a bit of a mess having to get up so early. Still we're here now, so you'll be on your way again soon and back in the old routine.'

Gill said her goodbyes to everyone and got in the car, she had to leave as she had a business appointment that morning. As she was driving out she put her head through the window, 'Well, hope to see you as you go through Wigan later in the day' she shouted and with a wave she drove out and down the road.

'Brew's up,' John shouted from the door of the van. Bill, Christine and I walked across, got in, sat down and looked around at one another.

'I'll be glad when we're finished.' Bill said as he came out of the bathroom with his gear on and his helmet in his hand. He looked a bit forlorn and I knew exactly how he felt as I was feeling the same.

'Look Bill, it's a good day today, you know the route from here as well as me, there are no big climbs, the weather's looking promising and if the winds favourable we'll have cracked it.' He finished his drink and looked up; he looked a bit more cheerful already I thought.

We lit a cigar each and took our cups and went out of the van, we all said our goodbyes to Christine who gave John a kiss, got into the car and drove off. After finishing the cigars we got on with the remaining jobs, filling the water bottles and putting the bikes that had been left in the van overnight back in the car. Not having a tent to take down it didn't take us long before we were ready to go. We drove out through the site gates and on up the A6 heading back to Beetham. It was a fair way, 26 miles to be exact. It brought back to my mind the day before, the fact that it had not been as good as I would have liked. I had been hoping to get to Preston at least but we were still 34 miles short, almost three hours cycling.

Before we knew it we were pulling up on the layby where John had met us just over 12 hours ago, it seemed a lifetime in one respect and like two minutes ago in another. We got out of the car and lit a cigar each, having got Bill's bike out of the car and mine out of the boot we got the wheels on and in no time we were ready to go. Finishing our cigars we put our helmets on and straddled our bikes. John got back in the car and started the engine. 'It will take me about half an hour to get back to the van, then I'll have to pack up etc., but it's going to take you two hours almost to get back down there, so I'll have a lazy morning and not set off until your well past.'

'Ok, we'll give you a bell when we are passing' I said. I looked at my heart monitor, it was 9.25 a very late start but we knew that it would be, so it was just a matter of making as good a progress as possible.

Hoping we would be refreshed after our so called break, we set off down the A6, heading for the delights of Carnforth. The A6 in this area is a good road for cycling on; there are no major hills of any note, after Shap it just undulates, Ok there may be one or two pulls that make you gasp but nothing you would lose any sleep about.

Before we knew it we had gone through Carnforth (six miles), Bolton-le-Sands (nine miles) and we were entering Lancaster, 12 miles from the start. Our legs were going well now, after 450 miles they were getting used to pushing us along at a reasonable rate. We entered Lancaster over the bridge across the River Ribble with the Ashton Memorial with its green dome in plain view on the top of the hill.

Lancaster is a very busy little city so it was good we arrived just before 10 o'clock, the morning rush hour had finished but there was still quite a bit of traffic about. We sailed round the one way system and fortunately as I know the place reasonably well, we managed to get into the right lanes without too much difficulty.

Having negotiated Lancaster the next place of any note on the agenda was Garstang about 11 miles away, which we arrived at no trouble. Unfortunately, this is where I had a brainwave. 'Look Bill,' I said, as we were approaching, 'if we cut through Garstang village and then Catterall we can cut half a mile off instead of going along the A6.'

Bill didn't argue, half a mile is half a mile at the end of the day so 'Yes that's fine with me' he shouted across.

So off we go branching left off the A6, down the hill into the town but it's Sod's Law, somehow we managed to get lost after the one way system. After we had cycled about for what seemed ages trying to find the road out we finished up going up a steep hill just to escape from the place. Finally coming out onto the A6 about halfway as far along as I thought we were going to and I would think taking about half an hour longer than if we had stayed on it. What Bill had to say about my great idea I will leave up to your imagination but it wasn't very complementary I can tell you.

As we got back on route I pulled over onto the grass verge, 'What's the matter now?' Bill enquired.

'Nothing, I'm just going to have a cigar and we can phone John, we're only a couple of miles from where the van is' I said.

'Great, I'm always ready for a cigar break.' He replied, putting his bike down on the grass. So we sat down on the grass and lit our cigars while I phoned John and told him our position.

'Good, you've made reasonable time.' He said when I told him.

'Yes the roads have been quite easy and the wind seems to have swung round in a favourable direction.' I answered; I failed to mention that our time would have been even better but for my 'short cut'.

Within five minutes we were on our way again heading for Preston, about eight miles further down the route. The towns and villages were coming thick and fast now compared to the first three days which made you feel you were getting somewhere. Preston was very busy as we went round the ring road with lots of heavy goods vehicles about and we seemed to get stuck at all the traffic lights. In fact, at one stage we resorted to something I would never do at home: mounting the footpath to get past about half a mile of standing traffic.

We weren't sorry to leave Preston behind, after all the beautiful countryside we had been through it brought it back to us how congested the North West is. From now on it was going to be built up areas and congestion for the next 30 to 40 miles until we got past the M56 and into Cheshire.

Following Preston we carried on down the A6 heading for Wigan, Bill's home town. Although I said we weren't doing too much climbing today the first 15 miles to Standish is all uphill but as the high point at Standish is just 350ft you do not really notice it. The next five miles, however, are all downhill, about 300ft and you do notice it because you can really belt along. In fact, we were just near where Bill lived, going down Wigan Lane, not far from Wigan Infirmary when we saw in front of us the massed crowds come out to see the local hero going though his home town. All three waved and shouted like mad but unlike the Tour de France Bill didn't stop he just waved back as just then we had really got some speed up.

As we were leaving Wigan centre just before the famous Wigan Pier, I signalled to Bill and we pulled over on a grassy area. I got off my bike and walked onto the grass putting my bike down. 'Cigar Time' I said to Bill as he came alongside me. Actually I had pulled up because my right foot had been getting hotter and hotter for the last hour or so and it was now that hot it had become painful.

I settled on the grass, took out and lit a cigar and then I bent over, took my cycling shoe off and started rubbing my foot. 'Are you all right?' Bill asked as he too lit a cigar.

'No, my bl**dy foot's as hot as hell' I replied.

'Why's that?' he asked sounding concerned.

'I don't know, but it's been coming on for a few miles, I can't feel anything when I rub it, hopefully it will be OK after a few minutes.'

Now, I know from looking it up in my cycling bible after I got back, that it is caused by pressure on the nerve, reduced circulation and numbness.

So although it feels like it is burning there is no actual heat involved. Ways to avoid it include wider fitting shoes, resilient insoles and perhaps moving your cleat position towards the rear a touch so that the ball of the foot is not directly over the pedal axle. Unfortunately, I must not have read that bit of the book so I hadn't a clue, I just had to rub it and hope for the best.

After the ubiquitous cigar break my foot was feeling better so I slipped my cycling shoe back on and got up ready to go. 'Are you OK?' Bill asked as he picked his bike up and had a drink from his bottle.

'Yes I should be alright now; I'll take it easy for a while and see how it goes.'

We set off down the road, passed Wigan Pier on our right-hand side as we entered the one way system around it. Going under a railway bridge we forked left following the signs to Warrington. Although much of the route so far from Preston had been through built up conurbations and not the most enjoyable cycling due to the volumes of traffic and the constant stopping and starting, at least it was relatively flat.

After leaving Wigan we passed Haydock Park on our left and reached the large roundabout at the East Lancashire Road and M6, Junction 23. Having battled with the heavy goods vehicles to get in the right lanes going round the roundabout we finally turned down the A49. The road going round Newton-le-Willows seemed to be a bit quieter and there were more green areas and trees than for the last couple of hours. In fact, as we headed towards Winnick it was quite pleasant in places, the part of Winnick we passed through I thought was reasonably picturesque, it had a large church up on the left and the half-timbered Swan Hotel just beyond. After negotiating another two large roundabouts, the second being the M62 junction 9 roundabout we were heading into Warrington.

The approach into Warrington is a very busy dual carriageway until you get almost into the centre. As Warrington is built around the River Mersey and the Manchester Ship Canal, it is at a low spot, so at least we had the pleasure of cycling downhill for the last seven or eight miles. In Warrington we followed the A49 signs heading south and swung round the large roundabout and over the River Mersey onto Wilderspool Causeway. Then at the next roundabout beared left to stay on the A49 towards Whitchurch, we were soon going over the old metal swing bridge that goes over the Manchester Ship Canal and heading up the hill out of Warrington.

Of course, having gone approximately 250ft downhill over the last seven or eight miles, we had now to go back uphill again only this time the 250ft was regained in just over a mile. As this was the only real climb we had to do today it caught us on the hop a bit. 'Bl**dy hell, that was a good pull.' Bill gasped as we got to the top. 'If I've been up here once in the car I've been up a hundred times and I can tell you it doesn't seem half as bad in the car.'

'No,' I managed to get out through the gasps for breath, 'After the easy day it catches you out a bit doesn't it?'

'Shall we have a cigar break?' he gasped.

'There's a layby at the top just before the Motorway junction, we can stop there.' I suggested.

So we cycled the next couple of miles and as luck would have it, there was John and the caravan pulled in the layby waiting for us. We pulled over behind the van and dismounted, leaning the bikes on the grass at the side of the van, we walked to John in the car and, opening the doors, collapsed into the car. 'How are things going?' he asked brightly.

'So far, so good. We knew it was going to be relatively easy today and tomorrow so we may as well make the most of it.' I took a cigar out of my pocket, lit it up and lay back against the headrest; Bill was sitting in the back. John turned to look at him.

'How are you Bill?'

He blew his cigar smoke out of the door and replied.

'Fine so far, that pull out of Warrington caught me a bit unawares but it was nothing compared to Scotland or the Shap.'

John turned back, 'How far do you think you'll get tonight?' he asked as he passed me the map.

'I had wanted to get as far as possible, but with the late start I think we will have to reduce what I was looking for.' Looking at the map I studied the A49 and took a leisurely pull of my cigar.

'What were you thinking of?' He asked.

'About 120 but we won't get that now.' I replied. 'There.' I pointed to Whitchurch. 'According to the cycle computer we've done about 70 miles, Whitchurch must be about another 30, so at least we'll get another 100 in which isn't bad seeing we didn't start till half past nine.'

John nodded, 'That ok with you Bill?'

Bill smiled. 'Sounds fine, can't wait to get there.'

I leaned back against the headrest and took another pull of the cigar, 'Well it should be pretty much plain sailing from here to Whitchurch.' I said closing my eyes for a minute to enjoy the moment.

We finished our cigars and got out of the car, John opened the boot and Bill and I swapped our water bottles for full ones. 'That should see us through today.' I said as we mounted the bikes.

'I'll just find us a place to stay near Whitchurch then I'll set off and get the van set up.' John said as he sorted the car. We got our feet into the cleats and waved to him and then we were off towards the big M56 junction 10 roundabout just up the road.

After the roundabout we settled down to a nice even pace along the A49, it's like a lot of Cheshire's roads, long, wide and reasonably flat with the odd short but steep climb with hedgerows and farmland along either side. Quite pleasant countryside but nothing that stirs the imagination, but having said that after the past few days of cycling we were glad there was nothing to cause any great excitement.

We were soon passing the white steel arch of Acton Bridge over the River Weaver where, on the left just past the bridge, there is a campsite. It brought back memories for me as almost 30 years earlier when my first wife Gwen and I had bought a ridge tent to go camping with the kids, we went there to try it out for the very first time. As we sped past, it made me wonder where all the years in-between had gone to and for a moment I was overcome with a melancholy and a sense of loss.

But when you're riding your bike trying to become an economical machine in unison with the bike, you soon get back to concentrating on what's happening around you again and feel your feet spinning and your legs powering up and down. The wind which always seems to be in your face whichever way you are travelling, is a bind so your mind is soon, one way or another, brought back to the reality of life even if it is an unnatural reality.

Soon after we arrived at the Weaverham roundabout, we swung right and just down the road was a sign saying Whitchurch 23 miles. The road by this time had become somewhat narrower, the villages of Sandiway and Tarporley were soon passed without anything of note happening. Although there was a short descent of 18 per cent with the resultant similar climb on the other side just after the sign for Cotebrook, this was followed just after the Portal Golf and Country Club by a mile long stretch where we went down a 10 per cent incline to the roundabout.

We went straight across the roundabout and carried on, the road had become quite decent again here so we made reasonable speed. It was getting quieter now that the evening rush hour was tailing off. We decided it was time we contacted John to see where we were stopping for the night so a couple of miles further we pulled into a bus stop just before some traffic lights. There was a sign pointing to the right saying Beeston and another brown tourist sign saying Beeston Castle.

'Right' says Bill, getting off his bike and leaning it against the hedgerow. 'I'll phone him.' I followed suit and lent my bike next to his.

'Ok, I'll just get a cigar out.' I replied as I reached round into my back pocket and fumbled for the packet and lighter. Unfortunately, there was no seat in the bus stop so I sat down on the kerb at the side of the road and lit my cigar. I could hear Bill talking to John and remember him repeating his words aloud for my benefit.

'At Whitchurch the A49 changes to the A41, keep on that road and go round the town until you come to a roundabout where you meet the A49 again, take the left fork and stay on the A41. In two miles go right on the A442, then first right into Green Lane the site is half a mile on your right.' He turned to looked at me, 'Have you got that Fred?' I looked up at him.

'Yes, it sounds fine, tell him we're just about past Tarporley so we have say 15 to Whitchurch say 20 to the site so should be there in an hour and a half.' Bill repeated it to John.

'Ok will expect you about 7.30 then, will get the G and Ts ready.' John replied, Bill hung up and got a cigar out.

'How are you feeling?' I asked as Bill sat down on the kerb next to me lighting his cigar.

'Not bad, seems a long while since we left home this morning.' I looked down the road to the lights where we were going to turn right and took a pull of my cigar.

'Yes it starts to tell now as the day goes on; we have over 500 miles in our legs. We are in uncharted territory here, our training hasn't taken us into these realms so were going into stamina levels you have never experienced before and I haven't for years.'

We sat there quietly and finished our cigars, then I stood up and started to stretch touching my toes once or twice to get my hamstrings stretching. 'Come on Bill let's get this show on the road.' Bill got up and stubbed out his cigar.

'What did you say? An hour and a half, I can't wait, let's go.'

We set off once again, got to the lights at the Red Fox and took the right, signposted A49 Whitchurch, Bunbury, and Beeston. We'd just got our legs loosened and a good rhythm going again, passing Bunbury and Spurstow when I got a call from Bill. I pulled over at the side of the road just next to a field gate, 'What's the matter?' I asked.

'A bl**dy puncture would you believe?' Bill shouted getting off his bike and looking like he was going to throw it down.

'Patience Bill,' I shouted, I didn't want him damaging his bike. 'We can't complain, we've done a thousand miles between us and it's our first puncture.'

I had a last drink from my bottle and the last piece of energy bar, lit a cigar and watched Bill at work. It didn't take long really; his wheel was off in seconds. A further minute or two to get the tyre and the inner tube off, check the tyre for any thorns or sharp things sticking through. Then it was on with the new inner tube, replace the tyre and within quarter of a hour he was pumping it up. I stubbed my cigar out as he was putting the wheel back on. 'See, no problem.' I said as I got back on my bike.

'No, not for you anyway.' He replied as he remounted and we set off on the last leg of our fifth day of cycling.

As it was getting late, instead of following the A41 around Whitchurch we decided on the direct option and went straight through the town. We were soon heading out of town for the A41, going over two roundabouts we were heading for the third, which I thought should be the one which split between the A41 and A49. Sure enough, after just one mile we hit the roundabout, staying on the A41 we carried on following John's instructions. As usual they were spot on and we arrived at the campsite without a hitch. As we pulled up next to the van it was just going on for eight o'clock.

John came out to greet us as we were dismounting, 'Bit later than expected' he said as he walked towards us 'Your ice has melted in the gin and tonics.' Leaning the bike against the van and taking my helmet off I reached in my pocket for the proverbial cigar.

'Mechanical problem, Bill punctured just the other side of Whitchurch.' I replied as I lit my cigar.

'Looks a nice site.' Bill said as he joined me in lighting up, 'Sorry we are a bit late,' he said to John, 'but you know what these breakdown services are like, never around when you want them.'

We sorted our bikes and gear out then went to the shower block. I stood under the constant stream of running water for what seemed like a lifetime. I walked back to the caravan feeling like a million dollars, that holier than thou feeling was really beginning to bite. I felt on top of the world and that everything was just wonderful, unfortunately it wasn't going to last.

I got back to the van and sat down, freshly shaved and showered with a gin and tonic and cigar in my hand all ready to go out for a lovely pub meal, I was ready to take on the world. Bill sat next to me with a gin and tonic and John on the seat opposite with a cup of coffee. (He was driving.)

'You don't look too excited John,' I said as I lay back enjoying my cigar and drink.

'Well,' he replied hesitantly 'it's like this, I've spoken to the guy at the farm and there's nowhere you're going to get a meal in a pub round here at this time of night.' I sat up and stared at him.

'What are you saying?' I asked, feeling Bill sit up next to me.

'The only place in the area he knows of is a Little Chef at the junction of the A49 and A41.' I stared at him in disbelief.

'You mean to say we have to eat in a Little Chef?' Bill asked.

'Well it's that or knock something up in the caravan.' John replied casually.

'Little Chef it is then,' said Bill, relaxing back against the seat smiling and having another sip of his drink. 'Always said they were fine places to take Gill for a nice romantic meal.'

We finished our drinks, stepped out, locked the caravan and got in the car. It was just starting to get dark as we arrived at the Little Chef, we walked in and got a table next to the window. 'Well what delights do you fancy for your dinner?' John asked as we perused the menu.

'How about a gin and tonic?' Bill asked as he studied the menu in front of him.

'Don't think you'll get much joy with that.' John replied, 'But you may get lemonade and if you clean your plate they may give you a lolly.'

We ordered our meals and in all fairness, I know I'm not fussy but the food was wholesome and tasty and cheap, what more can one ask? The waiter came up and asked us what we wanted to drink, but we had decided it would be cheaper and a better choice if we had a drink back at the caravan. So we settled the bill, left him a tip and set off into the night.

Getting back to the van we closed the blinds and put the heating on for a moment as it had got a bit chilly. John put the kettle on and put the coffee in the cups while I poured the gin and tonics, it was getting on for 11 o'clock. Bill and I lit a cigar each and I got up to open the roof light to let the smoke out.

'Well, what's the plan for tomorrow?' John asked as he lay back twirling his ice in the glass. We got the map out and opened it up, until now we had not really needed to look at the map as the route was obvious and tomorrow would be the same most of the way, that is until we got to Leominster. Then we would leave the A49 and start travelling across the country to Ledbury, Gloucester then heading for Bristol.

We got out the route that we had done during the planning in the winter and followed it on the map. It looked reasonably straight forward, the A417 then the A438 and back onto the A417 ring road around Ledbury and all the way to Gloucester. After that it was just a matter of finding the A38 in Gloucester then following it all the way to Bristol.

Originally I had planned to get through Bristol by the end of day six to enable us to have an easier last day and arrive at a reasonable time, but as we were still 130 miles away I knew it would be impossible. So it was decided we would get off as early as possible and just head down towards Bristol and see how far we got.

Bill and I finished our last cigars and we all finished our last gin and tonics and called it a night, Bill retiring to his tent and John and I settling down in the van. As I lay in my sleeping bag I consciously went over my body in my mind, feeling for any unnatural aches or pains. Everything seemed in order but I realised that with 550 miles behind me, with the effort and exertion I was putting my body through, something would soon start to tell.

As every other night, I lay and thought about Chris and the kids and wondered what sort of a day it had been for them, then offering up a prayer I was asleep before I knew it.

Day's Distance: 101 miles
Cumulative Distance: 552 miles
Day's Climbing: 1,978ft
Total Climbing: 14,143ft

Chapter 10

Day 6 Whitchurch to Stone
GOING THE WRONG WAY, BACON BUTTIES AND A BLISTER

The alarm went off at 5.45, I opened my eyes and looked round the van, John was just beginning to stir, 'Saturday and three days to go.' I said to John as he opened his eyes, 'Might not be as many big wagons on the road over the weekend.'

'No it should be a bit quieter in the morning until the shoppers get out around lunchtime', he replied.

I got up, went in the bathroom and had a good wash, got my cycling gear on and went back in the living area. John had got up, got the table out, put the kettle on and got the breakfast stuff out and then he went in the bathroom. I went out to see Bill, he was awake and had got up and gone to the toilet block for a wash already.

Later, sitting round the table we enjoyed our breakfast and nice hot drinks, thinking that they would probably be the only hot drinks we would have until evening. Having got ready when we got up, all we had to do was fill the drink bottles, put the spare ones in the car boot and load up with our energy bars. John would wash the dishes and sort the caravan, so we were ready to get away quickly. We got our bikes out of the car and the wheels on and we were ready for our sixth day, it was 7.25 when we finally cycled off the campsite.

John had given us the directions to get back on the A49 which were different from the way we came in. We turned left out of the site but at the next junction instead of turning right we turned left again. This brought us unwittingly out on the A41 lower down from where we had turned off the previous night. We turned right onto the A41 and within a few hundred yards there was a sign saying M54, Wolverhampton and Telford.

'Well, at least we're going in the general direction.' I shouted to Bill.

'It's no use going back now.' He replied. 'We would probably lose more time than if we carried on.'

His statement may well have been correct but failed to take into account the constant worrying about how or when we would eventually get back onto the correct route and how much further we were going to have to go. Having said that it was quite a pleasant road, long, straight and flat with farmland either side, in places it widened to a dual carriageway.

After almost five miles we arrived at the sign we were praying to see, it was a roundabout and to the right it said A53 Shrewsbury. 'Thank God for that' I shouted across to Bill. We were getting back on track, not there yet but at least heading towards the A49. The A53 was one of those good roads where they have a white line painted about 18in in from the edge of the road, like a mini cycle track. As the road was pleasantly undulating along the whole of its length, we cruised along with very little effort which got our legs loosened up after the efforts of the day before.

Eighteen miles from when we started, we finally hit the A49 just where it becomes the Shrewsbury ring road. We turned onto it feeling like we were welcoming a long lost friend even though we'd only been off track for a couple of hours if that. However, our feelings of joy at seeing our old friend (the A49) were soon replaced by feelings of concern as it became a very fast road and really busy as it was now taking all the traffic coming down from the A49 and coming off the A53.

After three miles on the ring road the A5 also joined us, so it got even busier; however, at this stage it had become a dual carriageway and the traffic was going like a motorway 70 miles per hour and more. Fortunately we still had our 18in on the other side of the white line to travel along, but I can tell you I couldn't wait to get off that road.

After a further three miles of the dual carriageway, we finally turned off the ring road and breathed a sigh of relief to get onto a more 'normal' road. The whole ring road experience had been approximately six miles or 20 minutes but it had seemed like an eternity. Bill who was riding at the front slowed down and I caught him up, 'Shall we have a cigar break after that, just to recover a bit?' He asked. 'That was a bl**dy horrible experience.'

'Might as well,' I laughed, 'mind you if you think that was bad wait till you get on the A30.'

'It can't be any worse than what we've just been through.' He said, as he lowered his bike onto the grass verge and got his cigars out.

'Well, perhaps not worse, but a damn sight longer.' I answered as I too put my bike down and got a cigar out. The weather had turned out nice again and the wind seemed to be more of assistance than on previous days. Although I must admit up to now we hadn't had any really bad windy days apart from the Shap.

'How far do you think that little diversion was?' Bill asked as we lay on the grass enjoying our cigars and having a drink.

'I should think it was no more than five or six miles extra.' I said, 'It's not going to make a great difference in the scheme of things, but I'd rather have done another five or six miles further tonight.'

After a brief respite we finished our cigars, got back on the bikes and set off, the road was really pleasant, no hills just gently undulating and going through lovely farmland, quite a contrast to yesterday morning going through Lancaster, Preston, Wigan and Warrington. Where there were buildings, they were just little villages scattered here and there in the countryside, not the large built up conurbations of yesterday. We made good time as we travelled along but in the distance we could see some ominous looking hills.

By the time we got through a tiny place called Strefford, the hills somehow were disappearing, where at first, it looked as if we had to go over them, the road seemed to be working its way round and going through a valley that could not be seen from a distance. A mile or so later and we were going through a lovely tree-lined boulevard which reminded me of sunny summer days driving through the lovely country lanes going down to the south of France.

Soon we were in the outskirts of Craven Arms; I had always thought it was an unusual name for a village. Apparently it was called Newton or Newtown but it now takes its name from the Craven Arms Hotel situated at the junction of the A49 and B4368. Again, unfortunately, there would be no chance of partaking of the fine alcoholic beverages no doubt available there.

However, before we got to the Craven Arms, just as we were nearing the sign for the railway station we could smell bacon cooking. Just in front of us we saw a café with a couple of tables and some benches and chairs outside. Without a word being exchanged we both pulled up outside the café, Bill looked at me questioningly 'Well what about it?' he said. I didn't need asking twice.

We both dismounted and walked into the little fenced-off area, leaned our bikes against the neat white painted fence and went into the Station Café. A smart looking middle-aged lady in a spotless white overall and white hat looked up at us and smiling asked what we would like. We both ordered a bacon sandwich and a mug of tea, taking our money she said she would bring them out to us if we wanted to sit outside. She didn't have any customers as it happened, but no doubt she thought if any did come in they wouldn't want to sit next to a couple of jokers smelling of sweat in the confined space of her café.

Going outside we took our sunglasses, helmets and gloves off and made ourselves comfortable on the benches. We both lit a cigar and settled down waiting for our breakfast treat. 'Well this is a quite unexpectedly pleasant interlude.' Bill said as he leaned on the table and took a pull on his cigar.

'Yes but we're going to have to make good time after the break to catch up.' I was constantly thinking of the distance to go and the time remaining and knew that though the break would do us good we would have to pay later.

After 10 minutes, just as we had finished our cigars the lady brought out a tray with the two bacon sandwiches and two mugs of tea on it, she put them on the table in front of us and went back in the shop. 'Looks good and smells good.' Bill said, as he took a huge bite out of the sandwich. I had a taste of mine; I had to admit it tasted fantastic. In no time at all we had eaten the sandwiches and lit another cigar each.

Leaning forward over the table I picked up my mug and had a drink, I shut my eyes and leaned back on the seat as I took a pull on the cigar, 'I feel like we could fly over the next few miles after this.'

'Yes, well unfortunately you'll soon get the chance to find out.' Was Bill's laconic reply as he leaned on the table flicking his cigar into an ashtray. 'How do you think we are doing, so far?'

'Well, I reckon we've done about 40 odd miles and it's what, 10.30 when we stopped. Say half an hour here and Bristol was 136 miles according to our planned route. With the best will in the world I can't see us getting within 20 miles of Bristol today.'

Bill looked up the road and drew on his cigar, 'No I couldn't see us doing 135 miles today, not after what we have already been through. It really starts to tell towards the late afternoon, your strength seems to drain away faster than it did at first.'

'Yes, well let's make a move or we won't be getting 100 miles in.' I said as I stood up and stubbed my cigar out in the ashtray. I put my helmet back on and once again the sponge supports in the helmet were wet and cold to my head, I leaned forward and pressed the helmet against my forehead and a stream of sweat ran out of the sponges and on to the floor. Bill got on his bike and we slowly set off, gradually building up the speed as our legs loosened up again after the rest.

We had no sooner set off than we arrived at the traffic island on which stood the famous Craven Arms, well with all due respect to the good people of the town I can't say I was impressed. I must say, and this is only a perspective from the outside mind you, but I can tell you this, I've been thrown out of much finer establishments in my time that haven't had a town named after them.

Well, after a couple of minutes we were out of town and back into the rolling countryside, and very pleasant it was too. We went past the sign for Stokesay Castle, 'No time for a visit today,' Bill called.

'Knowing our luck the Duke probably wouldn't be in anyway.' I said. This was unfortunately true but seriously it is well worth a visit if you are ever in the area. It's not so much a castle as a fortified manor house of which most of it dates from the 13th century.

The cycling was nice and easy, the next eight miles to Ludlow were gradual downhill, nothing excessive but enough to take the pressure off. In fact the next 25 miles only had two climbs of any note and they were only 200 to 300ft, the rest was long gradual descents. By now though, with the cycling we had already done, if there were any gradual gradients in the road we got over them without realising they were there, it was only the steeper gradients that had us struggling.

As the day passed on, the weather got nicer and I must admit I don't recollect a climb worthy of worrying about all day, it was a joy to cycle along taking in the surroundings, enjoying the countryside and we certainly made decent time as we pedalled along keeping a nice steady pace.

As we reached Leominster we turned left onto the A44, again we had got our 18in wide unofficial bicycle lane between the white line on the edge of the carriageway and the edge of the tarmac. At the first roundabout the A44 went left, we went straight on and were back on the A49, we carried on past the next roundabout until we came to the sign for the A417 Gloucester and Bodenham just after a Little Chef on our right.

After turning left we were on a nice country lane again, the only snag being with nice country lanes most of them are national speed limit, so cars do tend to have to brake hard when they see you, especially if there is another car coming in the opposite direction. On the grass verge at the side of the road was a sign saying Gloucester 32 miles.

I looked across at Bill, 'I reckon Gloucester is as near as damn it 100 miles so we must have done almost 70 miles now.'

Bill looked at his watch, 'It's 12.30 not doing too bad at the moment, fancy a cigar break?'

I looked at my watch; as if I doubted what he was saying, 'Yes, I think we are due a break.'

We pulled into a turning on our left that led to a farm gate, we both leaned our bikes against the gate; I got an energy bar out of my back pocket and took my drink bottle out of the cage. After a bite to eat and a drink I got a cigar out and lit up. 'Not a bad day today, the weather seems to be improving as we move down the country and the wind is more from the rear.'

'Yes, it's getting quite warm now' Bill replied as he leaned on the gate looking across the field smoking his cigar. Getting back on our way we made good speed along the A417.

Soon after our cigar stop we went past Hampton Court Castle, perhaps it lacks the small intimate charm of Stokesay Castle but you obviously won't need me to tell you about Hampton Court Castle and the many attractions it has to offer. Again all we saw were the gates as we cycled by on our way on what was beginning to seem like a never ending quest to get to Land's End.

The road is a brilliant road to cycle along: it's lovely countryside and farmland the whole length of it. As you get to a set of traffic lights there's a large timber framed public house painted black and white called The Trumpet. The signpost says Ledbury four miles, we turned left here on to the A438, in what seemed no time we were turning onto the bypass around Ledbury.

We were only on the Ledbury bypass for two miles, so in no time we were back on the A417 Gloucester Road again going through beautiful countryside, with the afternoon getting warmer I was beginning to get a sweat on. There were one or two humpy stretches before you got to the M50, then in less than a mile after crossing the motorway we saw John pulled up on the left.

We rode up to the side of the van and dismounted laying our bikes on the grass at the side. As we got in the car we left the doors open to keep it a bit cooler. 'Hi lads, so far so good?' He enquired, 'Just to let you know you're not the only ones who can take the wrong route, I went the wrong way out of a petrol station in Leominster and ended up heading for Brecon this morning.'

'Yes but it's not quite so bad in the car, you don't have to pedal to get back on the right track.' Bill answered, 'It's been another easy day today, just a bit warm since lunchtime.'

I lit a cigar and sat back, 'Have you any thoughts on where to stay tonight?' I asked him.

'Well to be honest at the moment no,' he said reaching for the map. 'Where do you think you may get to? That's the main thing. You're about 11 to 12 miles to Gloucester, 46 to Bristol.'

'Well there's probably nowhere in Bristol' I said leaning over the map, 'we won't get through the other side so it's got to be on the outskirt's or somewhere before we get to Bristol then.' I took another pull at my cigar and leaned back.

'I haven't been able to find a site convenient for this side of Bristol so it may have to be a CL' John said getting the Caravan Club book out of the glove compartment.

'That's no problem, if necessary we can all shower in the caravan, just take a bit longer that's all.' I answered as I started to get out of the car.

'What's a CL? Bill asked as we picked up our bikes.

'It's a certified location.' I answered, he looked blank. 'It's basically just a field that the owner has permission to have up to five vans on at any one time. It may have toilets and showers but most of them don't, there's just somewhere to get water and empty your toilet.' I explained.

We went to the boot of the car and recharged our drinking bottles then mounted our bikes. 'Right John,' I called, 'see you between 7 and 7.30.'

'OK, see you then.' He answered as he shut the boot lid.

Once more we were on our way, as always taking it easy at first until our legs loosened up again but this time we were on the final leg of the day. We soon hit the outskirts of Gloucester, as we went round the large island and started to head into Gloucester the road Over Causeway became a dual carriageway. Within half a mile we saw a sign for Bristol pointing right on the A430 so we got into the middle of the road and turned at the lights.

It was getting quite busy all the way into Gloucester by this time as it was now late afternoon, so it seemed a lucky chance that we were going round the outskirts of the city rather than through the centre. Within two and a half miles we were on the A38 and finally heading to Bristol on a good dual carriageway that, although very busy, we made good time. However, after another couple of miles we came to a large roundabout where we had to go three quarters of the way round and come off still on the A38 but here it had gone back down to single lane. The traffic wasn't quite as busy here as some had obviously gone in other directions at the roundabout and to make it more pleasant we were back in the countryside once more. It was just about here that John came past us sounding his horn as he went.

This part of the A38 was a reasonably pleasant road to ride, as the rush hour tailed away it got a lot quieter and as a bonus we had our 18in of tarmac to cycle up outside the white line, what more could you ask for?

We went through a couple of nice villages, Newport and Woodford. We had just left the latter and were entering a place called Stone when we saw John pulled up with the caravan in a layby on the right. We pulled over and got off the bikes.

'Hi John, we were just going to phone you to see if you had found anywhere, is everything alright?' I asked as I leaned over the car.

'Yes, fine, the only problem is the only CL I can find is quite a bit off route and it's towards Bristol. It's seven o'clock now; if it takes you another, say, hour to get down there we will be missing dinner again tonight. What do you think?'

It must have taken me all of a millisecond to think. 'Get the boot open, let's get this caravan set up.' I answered, 'What do you think Bill?'

'I've already got my wheels off.' He replied. So within a minute we were both sat in the car with our cigars lit enjoying the smoke.

It transpired that the CL was called Cliff Farm, at a place called Aust and what a view, it was situated between the two Severn Bridges. We got out of the car on the site and just stood there for a couple of minutes soaking it up.

'Come on,' John said 'we'd better get this caravan and the tent set up so you two can get a shower and we'll get out for dinner.' We all jumped to it straight away, Bill got the tent out of the caravan and started setting it up while we unhitched the caravan and got the legs down. John had kept some water in the barrel in the van so he only had to connect it up. As luck had it, the site had a couple of showers, so while John was finishing setting up the van Bill and I nipped off with our clothes and had a quick shower.

By the time we got back John had got the directions to the Boars Head at Aust, apparently a first-class eating establishment, so we put our washing gear in the van, loaded up with cigars and got on our way.

I wound the car window down, lit a cigar and started mentally going over my body. In general, I was feeling good. As we had ridden down I had got stronger as you do when you do more exercise but I knew that we had had two easy days and tomorrow was going to be a different kettle of fish altogether. It was noticeable towards the end of the day that my stamina was perhaps not quite what it was at the beginning but my main worry was soreness to my bottom which I had felt for the last few hours. I knew what it meant because the last time I had rode John o' Groats to Land's End I had the same from two and a half days out, the start of a blister.

So far although I could feel it, it had not formed yet so I had given the area a good wash in the shower, dried it thoroughly and put some antiseptic cream on, but we had two days to go yet and I wasn't looking forward to it. The last time the last two days had been agony but fortunately for me then, on the last two days we only had about 100 miles to do in total, this time we would probably have 200.

We got to the hotel and went in, it was quite busy as it was Saturday night but we found a quiet corner and got settled down. The waiter brought the menus, Bill and I lit a cigar each and we ordered the proverbial gin and tonics (John had a coke) while we were choosing our meals. We all agreed on garlic mushrooms to start followed by rump steak, chips, seasonal vegetables and onion rings with a bottle of Baron Rothschild, Mouton Cadet to help it down. Unfortunately, our poor chauffeur could only have one glass so Bill and I had to drink the rest of the bottle between us.

After the meal, which was excellent, we leaned back and Bill and I lit another cigar each while we all waited for our coffee and brandy. John just waited for his coffee. 'Well,' John said 'only two more days and roughly 210 miles to go. You were hoping for an easy last day I know, do you think you'll get it?'

I took a long draw on my cigar and blew it out in the direction of the extraction fan, 'Not a cat in hell's chance,' I answered, 'tomorrow's going to be a swine, the hills in Somerset and Devon may not be mountains but they're like the side of a bl**dy house and they come one after another.'

'Great!' said Bill, 'that's all I wanted to know, I'll sleep a lot easier tonight thinking about that.'

'You'll probably sleep easier than me.' I replied, 'Seeing I've got a blister starting and if it forms tomorrow I'll feel like I'm riding with a red hot poker up my backside.'

'Nice,' said John, 'just as I was wondering whether to have a Mississippi Mud Pie for my sweet.'

We got back to the van and put our feet up, John poured us all a drink (including himself this time). 'Right what's the plan then for tomorrow, do we know where we are going?'

Bill and I lit a cigar each, I reached over and got the route out that we had done when we planned the ride at the beginning. 'As far as I can see most of the route is straight forward,' I said as I opened the map. 'We follow the A38 all the way through Bristol, Taunton almost to Tiverton when we have to get on the A361, then in Tiverton it's the A396 to Crediton. That must be 100 miles of anybody's money, but I'd like to get to Okehampton if not Launceston if it's possible.'

Bill leaned back from the map and flicked his ash purposefully in the ashtray, 'How far is that then?' he asked taking a good drink of his gin and tonic.

'Well 120 to Okehampton, another 20 to Launceston.' I replied as I got up to get another round of drinks.

'Bl**dy hell Fred! You said it was going to be a hard day tomorrow.'

'Yes it is, but every mile we do tomorrow is one less on the last day.' I passed them both their drinks and sat down. 'You could be right,' I said remembering the last time I did it. 'OK we'll give Launceston a miss but I'd like to get to Okehampton if it's at all possible.' I lit another cigar and pondered on the problems of the next day while I stared at my drink. From what I remembered the last time the trip through Bristol was a bit of a nightmare but then we arrived during the Friday evening rush hour, I thought it may not be as bad this time going through on a Sunday, little did I know.

'Right, I'll start looking for a campsite somewhere around Okehampton,' John said as he studied the map. 'According to the weather forecast it's going to be a scorcher tomorrow down this neck of the woods.'

'That's all we need, still it's better than pouring rain.' I said as I lay back and relaxed.

'Right,' said Bill as he finished his drink and got up, 'if it's going to be a hard day tomorrow I'm getting to bed, see you in the morning.' He went out and shut the door quietly behind him.

Day's Distance: 110 miles
Cumulative Distance: 662 miles
Day's Climbing: 1,640ft
Total Climbing: 15,783ft

Chapter 11

Day 7 Stone to Whiddon Down
A FOOTBRIDGE ACROSS THE AVON, SIESTA IN THE AFTERNOON, DAMN HAWTHORN HEDGES AND LOST AGAIN

The Sunday broke a beautiful morning, we were up early and I went for a good wash, paying special attention to my backside. I gave it a thorough wash and drying before applying more cream, the last thing I wanted was a blister. Getting dressed in my cycling gear I decided to try two pairs of shorts, I hadn't seen this recommended in any of the manuals or magazines but I thought hell if one pair protects you two will protect you twice as much.

We had our usual breakfast, stuffed our pockets with energy bars and, of course, the cigars and lighters and filled our water bottles. Seven o'clock saw us stood by the car ready to go, as we got in the car Bill and I lit a cigar each and John came out of the van to take us back to Stone.

'It's definitely going to be hot today, it's only seven and you can feel it already.' He said as he got into the car.

We shot off back up the road, by 20 past seven we were on our bikes and ready to go. 'Good luck.' John called, 'See you the other side of Bristol somewhere'.

'Right,' I called as we set off up the road. I was feeling relieved that the pressure on my backside seemed less for wearing the two pairs of shorts; hopefully it would stay that way.

For the first few miles we took it easy as usual trying to get into our rhythm, also it was climbing for the first four miles. Once at the top of the climb I banged it onto the large chain ring and really started to push it as it was virtually downhill all the way to Bristol, today I was determined to get as far as possible to make it easier for us on the last day.

The road into Bristol was a dream, quite fast and hardly anything about at that time of the day. We sailed in, taking it in turns on the front our legs going like trains. Everything was going well; I was feeling really optimistic that we were going to get to Okehampton if not further when disaster struck.

I don't know what or how it happened but somehow we finished up way off track and like one of those people that you read about but can't believe who follow sat navs over the edge of cliffs, we blindly carried on hoping to get back on the right route.

Eventually we finished up crossing a large square that resembled a battlefield, with bars and fast food outlets all around, it was absolutely covered in rubbish, bottles and glasses a lot of which were smashed and fast food cartons. The natives had certainly had a wild night last night; it was that bad we finished up getting off our bikes and pushing them across this rubbish strewn wasteland.

After getting across we remounted and cycled on, not for very far, however, as we soon found our way blocked by the river. We leaned against some railings and looked up and down as far as we could see, to the left we could see nothing, to our right in the distance we could see a foot bridge crossing the river. We cycled along, dismounted and walked across a small very ornate cast iron suspension bridge.

'Bl**dy hell!' said Bill 'I don't believe this, how the hell have we managed to finish up like this? We must have wasted over half an hour bl**dy messing about like a couple of bl**dy nut cases!'

'Don't beat about the bush Bill; tell it as it is will you.' I laughed at his not too well disguised annoyance.

'Well, we've been giving it some hammer all morning just to throw the gain away by getting bl**dy lost.' He spat out.

'Look at it like this Bill, if we hadn't given it some hammer we would be further behind than we are now wouldn't we and we may still have got lost.'

He looked at me askance, when we got over the bridge we got back on our bikes. 'Well at least if my calculations are right we should be on the right side of the river at least.' I said reassuringly, but Bill wasn't going to let me get off that easily.

'Your calculations! How the hell did your calculations take us through that lot and look around us: God knows where we are now.'

I looked around; we were facing a St Paul's Church, the river was behind us so I thought about it for a second or two. 'Look if we keep heading south, we must hit the A38 somewhere because after the river it curves round to the west.' Bill looked at me, I could see he wasn't full of optimism, but finally he must have thought it beats going back, so grudgingly he agreed and we set off.

As luck would have it within 10 minutes, the first main road we came to was the A38, we didn't realise it at the time but when I saw a signpost for the airport I realised we were at least going in the right direction. Unfortunately after our good start that morning I felt we were now at least half an hour behind where we should have been.

We were going through a pretty drab industrial area of Bristol at this point and several times we thought we were on the wrong track but each time just as we were beginning to feel uncomfortable we would see another sign for the airport. Then just as we went over a railway bridge we saw a huge sign just before a road junction that said Taunton, Bristol Airport A38 to the right.

We swung round to the right and started to climb a sharp little hill, but feeling so relieved that we were finally on track we dug in and really climbed to the top. As we crested the hill I changed up onto the big crank again and dropped a couple of gears and really started to put some pressure on. Bill was tucked in just behind me as we forked right and came to a sign that said Taunton 41 miles.

Heading out of the city we had large areas of landscaping to either side and you could see to the north right across the river to the top of the valley on the other side. Within three miles from crossing the bridge we were out of the city and onto the national limit country roads. The climb out of Bristol was steady for about six miles but we kept the pressure on knowing that we had to make up lost time.

As we cycled along enjoying the morning sunshine and quiet roads we went past two large reservoirs, then in no time we were at the highest point and passing the airport, fortunately after the climb it was downhill or flat for the next 25 miles.

About nine miles outside Bristol just through a little village called Redhill I saw a layby and signalled to Bill to pull over. We pulled in and dropped our bikes onto the grass verge.

'Let's have a cigar break.' I said as I sat down on the grass.

'That getting lost in Bristol was a pain in the backside.' Bill said as he sat down next to me getting a cigar out. 'Talking about pains in the backside, how's yours?'

I lay back on one elbow and lit my cigar, 'So far so good, it feels fine at the moment.' I answered as I took a drink from one of my bottles. 'It's starting to get warmer already isn't it?' Bill looked at his watch.

'It sure is, by two or three o'clock it will be red hot at this rate. It's half past nine now and we've done about 25 miles, not too bad considering the cock up in Bristol.'

'No,' I replied rather distantly, as I lay there enjoying my cigar and thinking of home. 'We'd better get on our way soon; John will probably be passing us before long.'

As soon as we had finished the cigars we got back on our bikes and got going again, Bill taking over the riding at the front while I took it easy on his wheel. The A38 was quite a good road and though we passed through the occasional town it was mainly quite pleasant countryside. We were soon passing through Langford, a nice pleasant town with a couple of pubs, then we came to quite a large junction where you could go left to Bath or right to Weston-Super-Mare, we went straight on still making for Taunton.

We were about 13 miles from Bristol still 30 miles to go to Taunton. Bill looked at his computer, 'We've done 30 miles so far, say 30 to Taunton we should be there for 12.30.' He shouted back over his shoulder.

'It's 20 miles then to Tiverton, we could perhaps get some lunch and have a break then.' I shouted back.

Just about that time John came driving past with the caravan, we waved to him, as he went by he gave us the sign (alternating his indicators for a second) that he would pull up at the next available place. As it happened it was only a couple of miles down the road in a little village called Star and would you believe it he was parked on the car park of the Star Inn.

'It must be a craze down this part of the world.' said Bill as we pulled over and got off the bikes.

'What must?' I asked as I took the bottles off the bike to change them for full ones.

'Naming towns after pubs, I've never seen or heard of one before, now we get two in two days.'

John got out and opened the boot; we threw the bottles in and got fresh ones out. 'Glad to see you,' I said to him as he shut the boot, 'I was just starting to get a bit thirsty; I don't want to get dehydrated in this weather.'

'According to the latest forecast it's going to be very hot down here this afternoon.' He replied, 'I've kept some water in the bottom of the barrel so you can replenish your bottles if necessary.'

'Great idea,' I said as I reached for a cigar, 'We've only just had a break so we'll just have five minutes while we have a cigar then we'll be off again.'

Within minutes we were flying down the road, it was a beautiful part of the world, tree lined down either side or lovely farmland with mainly gentle hills. I kept the bike on the large 53 tooth crank and we made really good time. The thought of this being the penultimate day kept me going as I really wanted to put as many miles behind us as possible. As we travelled along we kept swapping lead position to conserve our energy but it seemed as if each mile we went it got hotter and hotter.

In no time we were going over the M5 and round the East Brent roundabout, then round another before going through Highbridge on the outskirts of Burnham on Sea. I looked at the computer it read 42 miles, looking at my watch it was 10.15, we were making up for getting lost in Bristol; if we could carry on like this it would look good for tomorrow.

Soon we arrived at Bridgwater, this was the first major built up area we had hit since Bristol and at nearly 11 o'clock it was reasonably busy. Bridgwater is where the road begins to climb again and although there are some good downhill stretches the road is constantly going higher for the next 60 miles.

Heading towards Taunton we got to Cross Rifles roundabout, 'I don't know about cross rifles,' Bill shouted across, 'looks more like a bl**dy cannon to me.' Sure enough as we swung round there was a large cannon in the middle of the roundabout.

'Couldn't leave something like that in the middle of the road round us,' I replied, 'it would be nicked for scrap within a week.'

Coming upon a large junction the A38 went left and we swung round to follow it. We were soon out of Bridgewater and the traffic thinned out, by the time we got through North Petherton we were back in the countryside and the roads were reasonably quiet again.

By 11.30 we were in Taunton, quite a sprawling town I think, which we entered on a quite narrow stretch of the A38. Then we came to a large junction, there was no sign for the A38 so we turned right following the sign for town centre, this turned out to be a much busier dual carriageway. After a mile or so we arrived at another roundabout that showed Town Centre A38 to the left so we breathed a sigh of relief knowing we were still on route.

Following this route the area soon got quite built up and before long we went straight across the road that leads to the town centre. Then we were finally on our way heading out of town. We forked right following the Exeter sign now; the road was quite pleasant with a lot of large trees giving us shelter from the sun that seemed to be getting hotter by the minute. Unfortunately, before long we had left the tree-lined boulevard behind and once again we had no protection from the sun.

Just as we were leaving the suburbs we went past a large pleasant looking pub on the right-hand side called The Stone Gallows, there were lots of people sat outside in the sun eating and drinking. It looked ever so tempting, I looked across at Bill. 'I know what you're thinking,' he said as we pedalled past.

'Yes it would be lovely to have a pint of shandy,' I replied, 'but hey, I've got plenty of water in my bottle what more could one ask for?'

We pressed on back in pleasant countryside once more with the occasional woodland stretch to give us some shade.

In one of the wooded stretches Bill signed and pulled over, 'Think it's time for a cigar, what do you say?' I got off the bike and leaned it against the fence.

'Sounds like a damn fine idea to me.' I said as I took a drink from my water bottle. 'If it keeps getting hotter like this we could really struggle, it's nearly midday now, by three o'clock it will be roasting.' Bill nodded in agreement as he took his cigars out of his shirt pocket and lit one. 'Look Bill, I think we should ride till say 2 to 2.30, then stop for lunch and have an hour or hour and a half off till the worst of the heat has gone, what do you think?'

Bill had a drink and a pull on his cigar and thought about it, 'Yes I think that would probably be the best plan, then perhaps we could do an extra hour tonight when it's cooler.'

'Good idea.' I said, but unfortunately even the best laid plans don't always have a happy ending.

After a 10 minute break we were off again, the road being a reasonably steady gradient and quite smooth we soon got back in our rhythm. From Bridgwater, through Taunton up to where we crossed the motorway a distance of about 23 miles it had been mainly uphill, but now after crossing the motorway it would be mainly downhill for 10 or so miles into Bickleigh.

Within a mile of the motorway the road crossed the M5 again and now we left the A38 and got onto the A361. After four miles we saw the sign for Tiverton pointing left on the A3126, we swung left and carried on. We basically skirted the town of Tiverton, the road staying reasonably level here as we followed the course of the River Exe.

The A3126 being a smaller carriageway than most we had been on since we left Scotland was quite tight in places but fortunately with it being Sunday the roads were pretty quiet.

As we entered Bickleigh we saw the car and caravan pulled up on the left on a large car park, as we cycled up we noticed it was the car park for the Trout Inn. We pulled in and cycled across to the van, I noticed the back legs were wound down. By this time the sun was scorching, I could feel it burning my arms and bouncing back off the tarmac. Getting off we leaned our bikes at the side and John came out of the van, 'I've got the kettle on would you like a brew?' he asked.

'Yes I'd love one,' I replied, 'But I'm going to have a shandy first. Do you want one Bill?' I asked looking across at Bill.

'I could kill for one just at this moment, with ice, of course.'

I got in the van took my helmet and glasses off dug out two glasses, a can of lager, a bottle of lemonade and a few ice cubes out of the freezer, poured the two drinks and gave one to Bill. Going into the bathroom I took my top off got a towel and wiped myself all over then got a fresh top out of my case. After having a long cool drink and a change of top I felt a lot better and got the cigars out.

John had got three chairs out and set them up in the shade of a tree just beside the caravan. We sat down and while Bill and I enjoyed our cigars we told John of our plans for the afternoon.

'Right, but just so that you know, when you set off just down the road there's a diversion, the A3072 to Crediton is closed. You have to go left at the bridge and up the A396 until you hit the A377 then follow that to Crediton.'

We looked on the map, the alternative way formed two sides of a triangle of which the third side was completed with the road we intended to go on that was closed. I worked out the distances it was six miles further.

'I know it's a bad climb out of Bickleigh but to save six miles I think we should risk going the closed way, what do you think Bill?' Being in the building trade all my life I knew it was very rare that the whole of a road would be shut off without the possibility of pedestrians getting past. Bill being a highways engineer agreed with me.

'Yes we'll be able to get past, no problem and if we can't we'll go through the woods to get round it.'

So that being decided we settled down, made some sandwiches and John brought the teas and coffee out and we sat outside and had a nice lunch in the shade while the temperature still climbed.

I got one of the seats out of the van and put it down in the shade and lay on it and shut my eyes. We had only got about 26 miles to do to Okehampton, 46 if we got to Launceston but I knew it was going to be hard graft with some inclines at about 10 per cent so I decided to get all the rest I could.

About five o'clock we decided to hit the road, we put our cycling gear back on and Bill and I lit a last cigar before we set off. It was still very hot but we decided we couldn't wait any longer it was time to move on. We had filled our water bottles; I had two on the bike and two in my back pocket for good measure.

We gave John a wave and told him we would see him later, the CL he had booked was between Okehampton and Launceston at a place called Lifton. That way we could head for whichever town we felt capable of reaching depending on how things went. It was going to prove an optimistic choice as it was nearer Launceston than Okehampton, still the idea was sound.

We cycled into the centre of the village and turned right in front of a large thatched pub called the Fishermans Cot just where the main road went left over the river bridge. We cycled up the road over another small bridge and round to the left past a beautiful thatched cottage following the signs for Crediton and Bickleigh Castle. Just up the road was a turning to the left for the castle, we carried on and this is where the road really started to get difficult.

The initial stretch of about 200 yards is at 20 per cent, it carries on then winding up between the trees at about 10 per cent gradient, even when it slackened off it was still about five per cent. I can tell you I was getting up those cogs as quick as they would change, my breath was coming in gasps and my heart rate monitor was heading upwards faster than I was pedalling. Having just started and not got back into the rhythm or our second wind we found it leg shaking, lung busting agony to keep going.

We soon arrived at the road closure and as we expected it left enough space to get our bikes through easily. After three miles we were cresting the top and starting the hurtling journey down again into the valley below. Apart from one climb inbetween it was four miles of constant downhill. We were just about to enter Crediton when the road started to go up again and from here on, as it turned out though we didn't know it, it would be going up for the rest of the day.

Going through Crediton it was quite tight in places and had it not been early evening on a Sunday I could imagine it being quite a busy little place. We got in the centre and picked up the A377 signposted Barnstable without any trouble and in no time we were back in the usual, rolling, hilly countryside.

We were soon in the quiet little village of Copplestone where the A377 bent round to the right and we kept on the A3072 up a steep little rise called Beers Hill. Though it was only half a mile long it was at five per cent gradient so after a long hot day you felt it.

We cycled through the village of Bow and out into the countryside once more, the temperature was still quite hot and the sun was starting to come lower down in our eyes. We had done almost 20 miles since we left John, I looked across at Bill. 'How about a cigar break? We've got about 10 miles I reckon to Okehampton, 30 to Launceston.'

'Fine.' He replied, 'We'll pull over there on the right.' He said pointing to a wide bit of verge just up the road.

He cycled across to it and I followed, as we pulled up I had one of those stupid inexplicable moments when you assume your foot is coming out of the clip like it has done thousands of times before only this time it doesn't. That was it; it seemed to take an age as I gradually fell to my right slap bang in the middle of the hawthorn hedge at the side of the road.

'Bl**dy hell!' I cried, as I slowly slipped further into the hedge each time I tried to push myself up. Eventually Bill had to get off his bike, I had to unclip my feet from the pedals and then hold my hand out while he laughed like someone not right, got hold of it and pulled me out. It seemed an age and dozens of scratches and thorns stuck in me before I managed to extricate myself from the hedge. Once back on my feet I picked my bike up leaned it against the hedge and straightened myself up feeling a bit sheepish. The only good thing about it was that no one had gone past, I felt foolish enough as it was.

We had a drink and an energy bar each then lit our cigars and stood there enjoying the early evening. It was still quite warm and I could feel the heat on my arms, legs and face, tomorrow we would be even more tanned. My double pair of shorts idea was holding up well, metaphorically speaking, at least my backside – though I could still feel the soreness – hadn't got much worse.

We took our time over the cigars, we were getting weary by now and not in any hurry to set off, it had seemed a long, long day. Finally we took the plunge, mounted the bikes and set off again. We came to a road junction that pointed straight ahead for Okehampton and left for Exeter and Launceston. For some reason, possibly tiredness, possibly because we had said we would try to get to Launceston I don't know but we turned left.

Travelling along going uphill constantly we became a little unsure as to whether we were on the right route or not. We crossed over the A30, 'We'll be riding up that tomorrow.' I shouted to Bill. He immediately pulled up almost across at the other side and looked down at the traffic flashing past, just like a motorway.

'You have to be joking?' He said in a quiet serious voice.

'No,' I replied 'that's our route now to Land's End.'

'I'll tell you now Fred, there's no bl**dy way I'm going up that road, there must be an alternative route.'

I looked at him, he was deadly earnest. I thought for now I had better take the easy way out so I replied, 'OK when we get back to the van tonight we'll have a look see what we can sort out.' It seemed to placate him and we set off again, but there was one thing playing on my mind, what the hell were we doing going over the other side of the A30?

We finally came to a village sign saying Whiddon Down; we cycled in past a little industrial unit and came to a road junction with a pub facing us called The Post Inn. I got off my bike and walked across the road, Bill followed.

'What's the matter?' he asked.

There were about 10 place names on various signs in front of the pub, none of them said Okehampton and the only one that said Launceston was pointing east and marked A30. 'That's going in the opposite direction we want to go, I don't know how far the junction for the A30 will be, but you wouldn't want to face that tonight anyway.'

'What do you reckon then?' He asked, looking at me as if to say this is your route so come up with something.

'Look, it's seven o'clock, I'm battered, scratched and boiled to a frazzle, I don't know which way to go, let's call it a day. I know I wanted to get further and leave us an easier day tomorrow but let's cut our losses and get some rest.' Bill agreed so we phoned John and gave him all the details on the road signs in front of the pub.

After a couple of minutes he rang us back, 'I think I know where you are but I'm not certain so you'll have to bear with me if I'm delayed but it should take me about half an hour. God, I thought, half an hour we must be miles from Okehampton even.

Now we had stopped, I was beginning to feel a bit chilly as you do when you've got a bit sunburned and it starts to cool down. We discussed the possibility of going into the pub for a drink but when we looked at all the expensive cars on the car park and looked at the state we were in, plus the fact we would have to leave the bikes outside made us decide against the idea.

So we just lit a cigar each and stood and shivered waiting for John. Once he arrived it was get the wheels off the bikes get mine in the boot and as usual Bill's in the back with him squeezed up against it.

'What happened?' John asked.

'Don't know really, one minute I thought we would make Okehampton relatively easily the next it had disappeared from the map. We'll have to have a look on the map tonight to see where we went wrong.'

As it happened the junction for the A30 was only a minute down the road, we swung on and Bill took the opportunity to have a good look as we were driving up at 60 miles an hour. Lifton, where John had sited the van, was about 22 miles up the A30 to the west. After half an hour we were pulling on to the CL; John had got everything connected up so we went and showered and got changed straight away ready for the evening.

Once we were washed and changed we walked up to the Arundell Arms in Lifton. I felt really good as you often do after a really exhausting day which wasn't caused so much by the distance we had covered, but by the constant climbing and the heat. What surprised me afterwards when we checked was that the total climbed was more than on any other day of the ride apart from the first day.

Knowing we had a really hard day tomorrow if we wanted to arrive at Land's End before Chris and our friends had to leave for home I had a light bar meal with a pint of cask ale and that was it. We got back to the caravan as soon as possible, while John poured the gin and tonics Bill and I poured over the map to see what had happened.

It transpired that if we had gone straight on instead of going left at the Exeter, Launceston sign the six miles we had travelled getting to Whiddon Down would have got us into Okehampton. Now when we went back to Whiddon Down to resume our ride we would have seven miles to go before we got to Okehampton. That meant we would have covered 13 unnecessary miles, I could have cried. We then poured over the map looking at ways to get to Land's End but at the end of it all Bill reluctantly admitted that it would have to be the A30.

We went outside the van with our gin and tonics and Bill and I with a cigar each, I looked up to the heavens and said a little prayer to God asking him to look over us tomorrow on what I knew was going to be possibly the most dangerous stretch of our ride. We finished our drinks and Bill got in his tent, John went in the van. I stood there for a few seconds longer looking at the stars as they were just coming out as the sun had finally set some time ago.

My thoughts went back to Chris, not at home now but only 100 or so miles away near Land's End. It was her last night in bed and breakfast at the farm they had booked and she would have to leave for home tomorrow. I knew she would have waited for me for as long as it took but Sandy and Dave had come down with her and they were in Dave's car and Sandy had to be back at work next day so I knew she would have to go at a reasonable time.

When I had phoned Chris before we went out to the pub I had said we hoped to arrive at Land's End by 7 to 7.30. After discussions with

Sandy and Dave she said they could wait until 7.30 but that would be it, after that they would have to leave for home. As I took a last pull of my cigar and finished my drink I made a quiet promise to myself that whatever it took tomorrow I would be there in time.

Day's Distance: 109 miles
Cumulative Distance: 771 miles
Day's Climbing: 3,691ft
Total Climbing: 19,474ft

Chapter 12

Day 8 Widdon Down to Land's End
PUNCTURES, MORE PUNCTURES AND THE LAST HILL

The final alarm sounds, it is six o'clock, and I am as stiff as an Egyptian mummy and sore, I don't know whether it's the scratches and sunburn from yesterday or just the cumulative effect on my body starting to tell but I ache everywhere. I get up wash thoroughly as yesterday and apply the cream to my bottom. I can still feel the soreness but I don't think it's any worse than the day before. Bill gets up and we drop his tent in no time, John has brewed up and got our usual breakfast ready.

I'm feeling more nervous and apprehensive than at any time since that first day which now seems a lifetime away. We don't hang about, I've got my two pairs of shorts on again and the bikes, bottles etcetera are in the car. No sitting outside enjoying a cigar before the off, today we have them in the car while we are travelling. Before we know it we are flying down the A30 back to Widdon Down. John pulls up on the pub car park, we pile out and in no time have the wheels on the bikes and are ready to go.

'Right,' said John as we were ready to set off. 'It's the last leg, I'll get back now and pack up at leisure as you'll be on the A30 the rest of the day. Good Luck.'

It was 7.15 as we waved to him and set off towards the A30. We passed the Little Chef and a Travelodge as we cycled the half a mile towards the A30, going down the slip road we were finally on the dreaded road. There was the usual 18in of carriageway beyond the white line which in the past had given us a feeling of security and we had been happy to cycle along but on this road it didn't seem half wide enough and to make things worse it was full of gravel and glass glinting in the sun.

We had only been on the road a few hundred yards when we saw the first sign, Okehampton 7 Bodmin 47. 'Well we are on a countdown now.' Bill shouted.

'Yes every sign we come to is one closer to the end, I can't wait till we see the first Penzance sign' I answered.

This first stretch was downhill so as it was reasonably quiet on the road I kept to the carriageway to avoid any obstacles in the gutter. Anyone who knows the A30 knows it just seems to be a series of long slow climbs followed by long downhill stretches.

After the initial downhill stretch when we first got on we struggled up the first climb, going over the top we put the bikes onto the big crank and jumped on the pedals, we started to fly down the hill dropping gears as we went. As we gathered up speed, I was halfway down when, bang! I had a rear wheel puncture. I shouted to Bill who was just in front, we eased to a halt and got off the bikes.

'Bl**dy hell, what a day to get my first puncture when I'm desperate to get to the finish for seven.' I shouted.

We climbed and lifted our bikes over the safety barrier onto the grass. I flicked the quick release and had the wheel off in a matter of seconds. Took the tyre off and got the inner tube out. Got a new tube out of my back pocket and within 10 minutes we were off again.

We had done about two miles and one puncture: not an auspicious start to the day, but before long it was going to get infinitely worse. We went over another two smaller climbs, the first about one and a half miles long at three per cent the second about a mile long not quite as steep, both relatively easy to get up.

Then 10 miles from the start we approached our fourth hill, it's two miles long about five per cent incline. By the time we're at the top we're in the bottom gear on the small chain wheel and I was pushing those pedals as if I was moving the whole earth. As we got over the top there's a two mile downhill stretch in front of us. As Bill is the better climber he's a bit in front, he gives a whoop of joy bangs his bike into the big gears and shoots off down the hill.

As he's always faster than me up the hills but I'm faster than him down I watch him go for a second or two then follow behind him, there's a bit of traffic passing so we both stay inside the 18in strip of carriageway. Fortunately for Bill his slighter frame allows him to get away with it, unfortunately for me my heavier build doesn't. I've not got quarter of a mile down the hill when, bang, bang, I've a double puncture. I scream down the road to Bill but he's flying, I scream again but no, he doesn't hear me.

I slowly pulled over to the side, get off and climb over the barrier looking down at my two flat tyres. I glance down the hill but Bill was just disappearing, great! I thought I only have one inner tube now, if Bill had pulled up I could have used one of his spares. I get the wheel off, the tyre off and the old inner tube out in no time. The new one is on and the wheel back on in five minutes.

I take the front wheel off and get the tube out and sit down on the grass, pump some air into the tube and start to try and find the puncture to repair it. That's when the problems start, with the weather being forecast sunny again I have got my cycling sunglasses on instead of my ordinary glasses. Result, I am as blind as a bat near to and just can't see where the puncture is. I pump some more air in and hold the tyre to my face and see if I can feel the air coming out, yes it's there! The elation I feel as I put my finger over the point where the air is coming and mark it with the crayon is unreal. After roughing the inner tube up with the sandpaper I get glue and smear it over the area, peel the back off the patch and stick it over. Great, I thought, I'll be back on the road in no time at all; putting the inner tube back in and the tyre on, I start to pump it up to its 100lb per square inch but for all my pumping it doesn't want to inflate. My heart drained, 'B**dy hell.' I swore as I pushed the tyre and saw my finger sink in, 'there must be another puncture somewhere.'

Sod it, I'm not taking the tyre off again I thought, I'll try and mend the other inner tube I took off after the first puncture. So I pick it up and start again pumping air in and trying to feel where the air was escaping from. After five minutes there was still no joy so I sat there frantic, wondering what to do, would Bill come back? I shouldn't think so, when he realises I'm not with him he'll probably wait for a while to see what happens.

Then it finally dawned on me, phone up John our support man that's what he's here for. If I phone he won't have left yet, yes that's the best idea get John to go into Okehampton and get me some more inner tubes and bring my glasses. Of course, when I think about it, it's only 8.30 the shops probably won't open till nine, damn! Anyway, first job phone John, but where do I tell him I am. I suppose he could go back to Widdon Down and come up the A30 till he found me but that would be wasting time.

I remembered we had just passed a junction at the crest of the hill so I decided to walk back to it and see what the signs said. I got up; put all the bits and pieces in my back pockets, slung my bike over my shoulder and carrying my wheel started walking back the way I had come. I soon got back to where the slip road joined the A30 and scrambled down the embankment to the road below. I walked 100 yards down the road to where the road sign was, sitting down I got the mobile out of my pocket and phoned John. He was surprised to hear me but I soon filled him in as to what had happened.

'Whereabouts are you?' He asked.

'I'm not certain but I think it's the first junction after you left us. The sign on the road under the A30 is the A386 Tavistock and Plymouth going south and Bideford and Okehampton going north.' There was a brief delay while he found it on the map then his voice came back.

'Right I've got you, now what do you want?'

'Get us four inner tubes 700 x 25 and another puncture outfit, just in case, oh and by the way bring my glasses will you, they are in the drawer in the front of the caravan.'

'Right, I'll be with you as soon as I can.'

I sat there distraught; I looked at my watch, we had started at 7.15 it was going on for nine and I had done 10 miles. I reached round and got my cigars out and lit one, let's calm down and think about this. I played the day out through my head; I had 104 miles to do at the start of the day that's 94 left. Looking back over previous days it has taken us say 11 hours to do 100 miles including breaks and a stop for lunch, say it takes John an hour to get here and another quarter of an hour to get back on the road, that makes it about 10 o'clock.

I sat in the sun and took a big draw on my cigar; blowing out the smoke and watching it fade into the distance I thought, that's nine hours to do 94 miles it's only 10 miles an hour without stops I can do that easily. Then I thought well perhaps not easily, the first six hours would be ok but then seven, eight, nine it starts to tell especially in my weakened state and knowing the hills between here and Land's End. I wasn't a happy bunny, but sitting there in the sunshine made me decide, if John did get back there in a reasonable time I was determined to do it.

John arrived coming in the opposite direction from under the A30, he drove past me then swung the car round in the middle of the road and coming back towards me pulled up off the road. I jumped up delighted to see him. He passed me the four inner tubes in the boxes.

'The guy in the shop asked me what size valves you wanted, I told him I hadn't a clue so he gave me these long ones, said they should fit whatever wheels you have on.'

'That's brilliant;' I cried taking them off him. I had taken the wheel; tyre and inner tube off again while I was waiting for him so all I had to do was take the new one out of the box and put it on, in five minutes I was ready to go. Taking the other three inner tubes out of their boxes I put them in my back pockets along with my glasses. John walked over and put the boxes and three old inner tubes in the boot.

'Look, I've spoken to Bill; he's miles up the road so he said he would wait for you. Do you remember that layby with the Greasy Joe's van on the top of Bodmin Moor?' I nodded, 'Well I've told him to wait there it's about 30 miles from here.'

'Right, I'll be getting on my way, I have a lot of time trialling to do and hopefully I'll see you in a couple of hours.'

He waved as I cycled up the slip road to get back on the A30. As I got on I saw the long, long downhill stretch in front of me. Sod it, I thought I'm not cycling in that gutter with all the stones and glass or I'll be punctured again before I get to the bottom. Traffic passing at 70 miles an hour or not I'm getting on the carriageway. So I pulled out, put it in the large crank and started to go.

I flew down the incline my computer touching 40 miles per hour before I got to the bottom. The descent easies off but carries on gradual downhill for about nine miles which was great to get me started again. As I got to the next uphill stretch I begin to feel the pull of the earth's gravity on me as I climbed, so I drop onto the smaller crank and try to keep my legs going. As I'm going slower I pull back over onto the 18in of tarmac on the other side of the white line, there's not too much gravel on it here and no point in taking unnecessary risks.

From Okehampton to the end of the A30 I always think of it as my L'Alpe-d'Huez but where 'The Alp' has 21 hairpins this has about 21 hump backs. I got my head down and I'm soon pushing my lowest gear, I feel like easing off a bit but I keep up the tempo, I have to get to Land's End by seven.

Before long I have reached the top and I start to hammer it down the other side, when bang, I don't believe it, I could cry, another puncture. I get off, swing the bike over the barrier and climb up a really steep embankment up to the top where it's flat. Ten minutes later, the tyre's back on and I'm sliding down the embankment with the bike over my shoulder. I wait until the road is clear, get back on the road and continue down the hill.

As I cycle along I quietly say a prayer, please Lord I'm not asking you to give me the strength, all I ask is to let me do my best and please, please no more punctures. I start another uphill slog, the hills are not desperately steep but they come one after the other and the cumulative effect starts to get to you.

This one is about a 400ft rise in five miles, then it's downhill for a couple of miles, then it's up again 500ft in the next five miles. I'm staying on the carriageway all the time now, if I can help it there won't be any more punctures. As I gain the summit of the next climb I am on top of the moor and there's about five miles to go to my rendezvous with John and Bill.

By the time I get there I'm absolutely shattered, I see the caravan on the car park at the side of the road and pull off the slip road and cycle round to the van. Bill's bike is leaning against the rear of the car, I get off and put mine next to his, I feel just about done in.

Bill and John are sat in the car with the doors open; I opened the back door and collapse on the back seat. John looked over the seat. 'You made it then? He enquired smiling, 'No more punctures I hope.'

I took a long drink from my water bottle, took my helmet and gloves off and wiped my face with a towel I found on the back seat, 'Don't mention it.' I said, I took a cigar out and lit it, the first one I had stopped for since I had left John back near Okehampton. When I had finished the cigar I took another drink and got out of the car. 'I'm going to go and get some lunch.' It was 12.30 I thought I had done quite well getting there so quick seeing that I had been on my own.

I walked over to the café van and bought two bacon sandwiches and a cup of coffee with a chocolate bar for afters. Going back to the car I put the drink down on the floor in the back and sprawled out on the back seat, it was a bit hot but nowhere near as hot as the day before thank goodness.

The bacon sandwiches soon disappeared so while I waited for my coffee to cool down I lit up another cigar. 'How have you gone on Bill?' I asked between pulls on the cigar.

'Great, I didn't know you weren't behind me for a couple of miles, I waited for a few minutes then decided to carry on for a while at a steady pace and see if you caught up, I thought you must have punctured again.'

'Have you had something to eat?' I asked as I took a drink.

'Yes we had something about half an hour ago.' Bill answered as he lit a cigar. 'It's been quite hard work along this stretch hasn't it?'

I put my feet up on the back seat and leaned against the far door. 'Yes and it's not going to get easier anytime soon, I mean this is the highest point of the day, so we're downhill all the way to Penzance but you still have intermediate climbs as well. Anyway, we'll just finish these cigars then we will be on our way.'

We got out of the car and put our kit on again ready to go, but this time we changed our cycling tops for blue ones that had Cancer Research UK printed across them. It gave me an incredible lift realising we were getting near the end. As we stood by the car ready to go John got out, 'Right lads you know where you're going today so I'll let you go for an hour then I'll shoot off and site the van near Land's End. Then I'll wait for you there; if you should need me give me a ring, OK.'

We waved and pushed off, as we got onto the A30 Bill said 'You take the front Fred.'

The section of road along where the parking area was is single lane and as you are on the top of the moor it's reasonably flat. You then hit a good downhill stretch and the computer is touching 40 again as you fly down from the top of the moor. In fact, apart from a couple of slight rises it's basically downhill for about nine miles to just south of Bodmin.

After reaching the bottom near Lanhydrock it's then an undulating grind for the next six miles until you are approaching the A39 junction when the road really starts a long drag up. By the time I was at the top my legs were almost ready to give up, I made a conscious effort to ease back on the pace I was going, especially up the hills. As we cruised along the top for a mile or so I managed to recover from the exertion of the last climb and get my breath back.

Then imperceptibly at first the road began to drop again, I looked up into the distance and saw that it was falling gradually as far as we could see. I put the bike onto the large crank and onto the middle cog at the back and started to put a bit of speed on as I shouted back to Bill. 'We won't go too hard down this stretch, we'll try to conserve a bit of energy, because as you know there's always another hill.'

'Ok I'm behind you,' he called, as we started to build up speed. The downhill was about four miles but unfortunately, long before we got to the end we could see the road rising up again in the distance. At first it didn't seem too bad but as we got further into the bottom of the dip and then started the long slow climb up it seemed to get steeper and steeper.

We arrived at a road sign which had printed at the top 'Highgate Hill', the turn off was for Newquay, St Columb, St Dennis and Indian Queens. By the time we hit the slip road I was in my bottom gear and on auto pilot. It wasn't that these hills were steep, but for me who had only started cycling properly again six months ago after a four year layoff and with 800 miles behind me in the last eight days it began to tell with a vengeance.

When I really started to get desperate, the thought of Chris waiting for me at Land's End somehow kept me going. Then just before we reached the top I looked up and there in front of me was a road sign and among other places, there right at the bottom it said Penzance 35 miles. My heart lifted, all at once I had a sudden input of energy and I felt lighter and fresher. The road went up for another few hundred yards and when I got over the top I could see for miles, we were approaching a huge descent. As we headed over the crest we saw a sign showing downhill eight per cent incline.

Feeling buoyed by the Penzance sign and then seeing the steep downhill in front of me and the plain stretched out below I stood on the pedals and started to go, as I picked up speed I gradually put it into the biggest gear I had. The wind started to fly past me, I got down onto the drops and gave it everything I could, the computer gradually went up, 35, 40, 45, and 50, it went over 50 and as it did the bike started to vibrate; 52, 53, the vibrations started getting quite bad. Common sense or fear, I'm not sure which was the driving force, made me gradually ease off the pedals, as it dropped under 50 the vibrations stopped and I carried on down the remainder at a nice 45 miles an hour until we got to the bottom.

After that we had a couple more climbs in the next 10 miles and then it was virtually downhill until just past Camborne. We soon got to the Loggans Moor roundabout signposted for Angorack, when I get there in the car I start to think that I've almost arrived, but that is usually when I'm going to Penzance but today we would have another nine miles to cover. However, it still made me feel great, especially when you go round the roundabout, and start climbing and see the road sign saying Penzance nine miles.

Bill got up just behind me and shouted, 'Only nine miles to Penzance, how many to Land's End?'

'About 18,' I shouted in between gasps for breath as I climbed the long drag up from the roundabout.

As we went under the old railway bridge we saw a sign for a layby. 'Fancy pulling in for a cigar?' Bill shouted from behind.

'No we'll break its back first, once I know we are going to get there in time then we can sit back and enjoy one.' I was determined I was going to get there for seven o'clock and, after a disastrous start, it was beginning to look good.

Once we had got to the top of the hill it was a breeze, four miles gradual downhill all the way to Penzance. We got to the Long Rock roundabout where the sign said Penzance two miles, Bill shouted, 'not far now, we'll soon be there.'

'Well, not exactly soon.' I replied as we pressed on, we got to the next roundabout where the little retail outlet is, then we were going past the heliport. Over to our left we could see St Michael's Mount beautiful and clear in the sunshine, but we had to concentrate on the road as it was a dual carriageway and we had to get into the right-hand lane at the next roundabout.

Spotting a gap in the traffic, we stuck our right hands out and moved over to the centre of the road. We cycled round the roundabout and took the second exit signposted West Cornwall Hospital. In front of us was yet another climb, 'Gordon Bennett' Bill gasped as we dropped into our lowest gears and crawled up, 'there can't be any more hills after this surely.'

'Bill, how many times have I told you, there's always another hill,' I shouted back.

It was as if we had paced our bodies to the point of collapse after 873 miles and here we were 10 miles short and our energy reserves were just running out. As we got to the top of the hill a mile closer to the finish we saw the sign for Land's End just before a second roundabout.

We swung round the roundabout and just on the other side was a large expanse of grass, Bill pulled onto the grass, dropped his bike and lay down next to it. 'Cigar break?' He said as he looked up at me, I looked at my watch it read five o'clock.

I dropped my bike and, taking my helmet off, sat down next to him. 'I think we've done bl**dy well today considering all the punctures. If we have a break here it will give us a chance to get up that last hill and we should be there for half six.'

Bill sat bolt upright and stared at me, 'What did you say?'

'I think we've done well today we should make it for about half six.' I answered as I got my cigars out.

'No not that,' he almost shouted, 'the other.'

'What other?' I asked wondering what the hell he was getting excited about.

'The last hill! You said the last hill.'

I couldn't help smiling, we seemed to have lived with it for an eternity: 'There's Always Another Hill' had become our phrase, our philosophy, it had shared our journey with us through the good times and the bad. I lit my cigar and looked at him, 'Don't be daft, I didn't mean it literally you fool, everyone knows, there's always another hill.'

We both lay there quietly thinking our own thoughts, I phoned Chris, she was at the finish waiting with John, Sandy and Dave. 'Get the champagne on ice; we'll be there in about an hour.' I said.

'We can't wait,' she replied, 'I've missed you.'

'I've missed you too, see you soon.' I hung up, 'Come on Bill it's the last leg, one more struggle and it's downhill all the way.'

We got up and on our bikes for the last time, for some reason after all this way Bill went to the front, perhaps he felt sorry for me after doing the lead for the last section. We cruised down the nice road with lovely trees either side and grass verges. As we got past the third roundabout the wide road went into more of a country lane with tall trees either side of the road sheltering us from the sun. You could smell the fresh air and the countryside, it took you back all those years, distant memories from your childhood, everything seemed great.

As we went past the road junction that had Newlyn to the left, St Justs to the right the road began to climb, gently at first but as we went further it got steeper. In no time I was in my bottom gear and crawling up, and in truth after the day I'd had, it was a hill too far. I rocked from side to side; my head was down, my breath coming in long drawn out gasps. The sweat ran down my face and arms and dripped off onto the road as I dragged my way up the three miles to the top. If this had not been the last few miles, if it had been two days ago I think I could have got off and called it a day.

I vaguely remember cycling into a little village called Drift, the road still went on for what seemed forever upwards. I struggled on for what must have been about a couple of miles which seemed like 100. When I looked up and I could see the road disappear and spread out before us in a huge panorama, all the surrounding countryside 200ft below with the sea in the distance. Then as we went over the top the gravitational pull of the earth started to pull me downwards, I gradually dropped gears until I was on the big chain ring and my highest gear.

We sped along the twisting country lanes; even the one or two slight rises we had to go up didn't seem to affect us. We were finally heading for that finishing point, the adrenalin was pumping and nothing was going to stop us now. I could feel the wind in my face with the speed we were going, the cycle computer said 30 miles an hour and I had a double take when I saw it. It's usually downhill when I get up to 30, but with the wind behind us we were flying and I was certainly pushing every last ounce of energy into the pedals to keep that big gear going round.

As we sped through the lanes I had become conscious of a car behind me, I realised he must have been trying to get past for some time. But as he gained on us on the short straights we were pulling away from him through the bends. However, we eventually came to a longer bit of straight road and I put my hand up and waved him through.

We saw the sign for Land's End village and pressed on, the emotions that course through you when you realise you're so close are amazing. I didn't feel the tiredness or soreness any more, all I felt was an ecstasy that one more bend and we would be there.

Yet underneath it all, as I drove on keeping my legs pumping, keeping the speed up, was a feeling right in the core of me, so deep you could call it in my soul; a feeling that when it was all over, when we had finished there would be a sadness, something would be missing.

We shot past the First and Last pub and then, though we didn't know it at the time, the campsite that John had sited the van on. We swept round the last bend; the buildings on Land's End came rapidly into view shining white in the sunshine.

The very last stretch is a slight downhill, I drove those pedals round as fast as I could, I thought there's no point saving any energy now. It was as if it was cathartic spending every last drop of energy as we drove on until the very last moment when we braked and pulled up outside the little white domed entrance kiosk to Land's End.

As we stopped the guy in the kiosk looked us up and down, 'End to Enders?' he enquired.

'Yes,' was the single word reply, there wasn't too much else to say, I just wanted to finish.

'How long has it taken you?'

'Eight days.' I answered.

'Your mate's arrived; he's waiting for you over there.'

'Yes I can see him.' I gasped, looking down the road I could see them all waiting for us, I just wanted to get down that last 100 yards, get off my bike and get hold of Chris.

'OK, off you go.' He said with a smile. Then, just as we were about to set off, I heard him say, I don't know whether it was to himself or not. 'Bl**dy fools should have more sense at your age.'

I couldn't care less, I was off, cleats in pedals and away at last. I hadn't gone five yards when Bill shouted, I braked and circled back round to him. 'What is it?' I needn't have asked, he was just getting off his bike and I could see his chain had come off. I looked at him in despair, 'Nearly 900 miles, 100 yards to go, what a time for your chain to come off.' Whether it was the excitement of finishing or what I don't know, but it seemed to take an inordinate amount of time for him to get the thing back on.

Finally the chain was on again, we were on our bikes once more and we slowly cycled the last 100 yards and finally crossed the white line with the word 'FINISH' written along it. There was a crescendo of clicking and flashing cameras taking photographs of the heroic pair, as we cycled across, well there were three anyway.

I looked at my watch it was 20 past six, I was ecstatic! I got off the bike, walked over to John, shook hands and then we hugged one another. I went across to Chris and held her tight towards me and gave her a kiss, it seemed an eternity since I had held her, not just four days ago when I said cheerio as I left to go back to Beetham. I went and shook hands with Dave and hugged Sandy and gave her a kiss.

We walked together down to the End to End office, leaned our bikes against the wall and the three of us went in leaving the others to look after the bikes. We gave the guy sat at the desk all the details of our trip, showed him the record card we had got signed a lifetime ago in John o' Groats and some photographs John had got as soon as he arrived at Land's End. He remembered that from the last trip when we had to wait about for an hour to get the photographs developed to prove we had done it.

He filled in the record book with our details, the details of our trip and the three of us signed it, he shook our hands and congratulated us and that was it. As we came out and picked our bikes up to walk down to the finger post for the photographs a guy stopped me just as I was about to set off. 'Have you two just ridden in here about half an hour ago?' He asked.

Wanting to catch the others and crack open the bottles of champagne, I was going to give him short shrift but I was in too good a mood so I just replied yes, wondering what the hell he wanted.

'Right, well I followed you quite a bit of the way in, I couldn't get past you.'

I looked at him, but he didn't seem to be being funny so I just said, 'Oh I'm sorry about that, but it has been a long day and I just wanted to get finished.'

'Oh that's alright', he said in a cheery voice, 'do you know you were doing over 30 miles an hour at times?'

'Was I?' I replied, 'I can assure you it's not been like that all the time, some of the time I think I've done well to do three miles an hour.'

He looked at my Cancer Research t-shirt and getting his wallet out he took out a £10 note and gave it to me. 'Well here you are and congratulations I hope you have raised a lot of money for a worthy cause.' I reached out and took the proffered note.

'Thank you.' Was all I could say with a lump in my throat, this guy whom I had almost shot down for delaying me getting to my celebration drink; a guy I didn't know from Adam just stopped me and handed over a tenner for Cancer Research. It just goes to show that most people who you come across are really nice and a few seconds of your time costs nothing.

I hurriedly caught up with the others and we made our way to the finger post, this time, unlike seven in the morning in Scotland, the photographer was there. Chris and Sandy opened a bottle of champagne each and got six glasses out, they had come prepared, they gave one to John, Bill and I and they had one each. They poured out the champagne and we all drank to our success.

Chris, Dave and John only had one small glass each as they were going to be driving back so between the two bottles it left plenty for Sandy, Bill and I. The three of us then went down to the photographer and had our photographs taken, of course while the photographer was doing his bit Chris and Dave were taking photographs as well.

Afterwards as we sat about on the rocks talking, Bill phoned Gill to let her know we had arrived, she was over the moon when she heard his voice, you could hear her excitement over the phone from where we were sitting. I suddenly felt sorry for Bill and John that Gill and Christine weren't there to share in our celebrations, although no doubt they would both have a little celebration in their own way at home.

All too soon it was time to say cheerio to Chris, Sandy and Dave, we walked with them to the car park. As I watched them going up the road, I felt lonely and it was a bit of an anticlimax, reaching into my jersey I got a cigar out and lit it. 'Well I suppose it's time we got to the van and had some dinner it will be a long day tomorrow.' It seemed odd without the thought of having to get up and spending a day on the bike again tomorrow, as if a way of life I was familiar with had come to an end.

'Come on,' John said, 'Let's get to the car and get off, we have some more celebrating to do or would you prefer to cycle back to the campsite?'

I won't tell you what we said in reply other than say we all walked across to the car, took the wheels off the bikes, I put mine in the boot and Bill squeezed into the back seat with his for the final time.

John had sited the van at a place called Seaview Holiday Park, it was half a mile from Land's End itself, so we were only in the car a couple of minutes before we were piling out. Bill and I took our wash bags, towels and clothes and walked over to the showers. By the time I had stood under the shower relaxing for about 10 minutes, got washed and had a shave it was about eight o'clock.

We walked back to the caravan, John had put Bill's tent up earlier in the day and now got the chairs and tables out and poured three gin and tonics, 'Here you are lads, put your feet up and have a drink then we can go and get something to eat.' We all sat down, Bill and I lit a cigar each and sat back to unwind, it seemed odd knowing you didn't have to get on your bike again tomorrow, like something was missing.

Bill sat up suddenly, 'What are you doing for dinner then?'

'Thought we may as well go to that pub just up the road, The First and Last, you must have seen it on the way in.' John replied as he took a good drink of his gin and tonic.

'If you don't mind I'll give it a miss and have an early night, I don't feel very hungry and I'm shattered?'

'No by all means, are you alright?' I asked him, feeling a bit concerned.

'Oh no I'm fine, just shattered. In fact, if you don't mind I'll take a nice nightcap with me.' So he went into the caravan got a pint glass and filled it up with gin and tonic.

'Some nightcap that is.' John said as Bill crawled into the tent.

'See you in the morning, what time are we getting up?' Bill asked as he was getting into his tent.

'When we wake,' I replied, 'If you're up before us you can always go for a spin on the bike.'

'Yeh, I can see me doing that tomorrow morning, goodnight.'

John and I got up and put the chairs in the van; we locked the caravan and started walking up the road. It was only a couple of hundred yards, we got inside and it was packed, I went to the bar and ordered two pints. While the young lady was pulling the pints I asked if the restaurant was open.

'Oh no, we stopped serving at eight I'm afraid.' She said smilingly as she reached out to take our money.

'I don't believe it.' I said to John as I looked at my watch, it was just about 8.25.

John took a drink of his pint and looked at me, 'What do we do now then do you reckon? By the time we get anywhere else they'll have stopped serving too I should think.'

'Well, we have plenty of stuff in the van for emergencies; if we go back we can knock something up ourselves in half an hour.' I said as I looked into my glass watching the bubbles rise slowly to the surface.

'Come on then, we'll drink up and get back to the van, at least we will have somewhere to sit.' John empted his glass and put it on the bar, I followed suit and within five minutes we were back in the caravan.

From the cupboards I selected a tinned steak and kidney pie, tinned new potatoes and a tin of peas. I put the oven on to warm up and the potatoes and peas in a saucepan each on the hobs. After five minutes the oven had warmed up and the pie was in, I put the potatoes and peas on under a low light and sat down.

We had a couple of gin and tonics and I had a cigar while we waited for dinner. We talked quietly about the day so as not to disturb Bill who still had his light on in the tent we noticed when we got back. Soon everything was ready; we set the table up in the middle of the van and got the plates, knives, forks and condiments out. I dished the food out and we settled down to enjoy it and I must admit it was quite tasty, even if I do say so myself.

After dinner we washed the pots and put them and the table away, before sitting down for a nightcap. John poured the gin and tonics while I put my feet up, opened the window wide and lit a cigar. 'Well we made it in time at the end.' I said as I lay back and blew the smoke out of the window.

'Yes, I didn't think you would after those punctures.' He replied as he put his feet up as well. We sat for another 10 minutes each in our own thoughts until I had finished my cigar and we both finished our drinks. I got the sleeping bags and pillows out and we settled down on our respective sides. 'Well John, thanks for everything you've done for us, we would never have made it in the time without you.'

'That's alright, I've enjoyed every minute of it, wouldn't have missed it for the world. See you tomorrow.' With that it was over I said a quick prayer and fell asleep.

Day's Distance: 102 miles
Cumulative Distance: 873 miles
Day's Climbing: 3,425ft
Total Climbing: 22,899ft

Chapter 13

The Ribble Valley Ladies Luncheon Club
LONG DRIVE HOME, FROM HERO TO ZERO BUT A GOOD DAY OUT

The next morning I woke up on my own without the alarm going off, opened my eyes slowly, lay in bed and mentally went all over my body, to my amazement I felt really good. I looked at my watch it said 7.15, I shut my eyes again and for a moment I just lay there slowly coming round in the wonderful warmth of the knowledge that I didn't have to rush up and get up and get on that bike again. After quarter of an hour I got up and put the kettle on, John woke up and looked at his watch. 'Fancy a brew?' I asked as he lifted the blind a touch to peer out.

'Yes that will do nicely.' He replied as he lay back.

I did us all a brew, threw some clothes on and took Bill's out to him; he was still asleep but woke as I opened the tent zip. 'Got a brew for you mate, thought we would have a nice relaxing drink before we went for our showers. No need to be up early this morning.'

He took it off me gratefully and passed me the now empty pint glass that had been full of gin and tonic just about 11 hours ago. I went back in the caravan, John had got dressed and was drinking his tea. I joined him and we exchanged small talk while we had our drinks. I opened the window and lit a cigar. 'Good job you've finished your ride you've almost run out of cigars.'

'No doubt our support driver would have sorted it while filling up with petrol.' I replied, 'You know, if we had taken the cigar stops out we would have more than likely finished a day earlier.'

'Yes but it probably wouldn't have been as enjoyable' he said smiling.

'Who the bl**dy hell enjoyed it?' I laughed. 'Only someone not right in the head would have enjoyed that last week.'

After having our drinks we all strolled to the shower block, got showered and went back to the van for breakfast. We kept to our normal breakfasts that we had eaten all week but it seemed strange sitting there in jeans and casual tops after the eight days of sitting in cycling gear.

After breakfast we dismantled Bill's tent and put it in the caravan along with his bike, while I left mine in the boot of the car. This time John had us to help him pack up the caravan, so in no time at all we were all set up and ready to move off. We hitched up and had one last look round to make sure we had not left anything, checked the lights on the caravan and we were away by 10.15.

Sitting in the front of the car as we went back up the A30 I lit a cigar and gazed through the window, thinking about struggling up the hills we were flying down now at 55 to 60 miles an hour, was it only yesterday? Sometimes it seemed like a lifetime ago then, at other times, it seemed as if it was only yesterday.

We motored along and it was as if every mile, every hill had memories. To this day every time I go along not only the A30 but any section of the road that we covered over those eight days, I still remember with a fondness the good times we had. The laughter and jokes, as I said the mind doesn't often bring back the pain, thank God. Yet at the time we were doing it I never dreamt for a minute during all the effort, pain and suffering that I would look back on it with a kind of nostalgia, even now the best part of 10 years later I don't know how to describe it.

John kept a steady speed going and we flew through the places we had struggled over yesterday. The signposts brought everything back to me, Camborne, Indian Queens, Bodmin and, of course, Launceston. As we passed on the other side, I looked across at the place where I had the double puncture. I remembered the sick feeling I had when I started to think it wasn't going to be my day, that I wasn't going to get to the finish in time to see Chris. Soon, however, we were past the junction where we got on the A30 and flying up roads we had not come along. I thought for the time being I could put the memories away for a while, but it didn't work out like that.

We had been on the road just over two and half hours, had done about 120 miles and were at Exeter services at junction 30 on the M5. We decided to stop for a quick lunch at the services and to give John a longer break I took over the driving when we got back to the car. Over the last 10 days John had driven the best part of 1,700 miles and I thought he could do with a break. As I cruised up the motorway a bit slower than John doing a steady 55 miles an hour all the time my thoughts were wandering, I seemed to be reliving parts of the ride in my mind. After another 100 miles we pulled in at the Michael Wood services for another break after which John got back behind the wheel to finish off the remainder of the journey.

After my spell driving, I got in the back seat and let Bill sit in the front with John. I got a cigar out, stretched out across the back seat and opened the window. Lighting my cigar I sat and watched the smoke swirl slowly upwards until it was caught by the draught from the window, then rapidly sucked outside.

I shut my eyes and listened to John and Bill chatting in the front, subconsciously I felt over my body. My arms and torso felt firm as if the fat that used to cover it had gone as indeed a lot of it had. I felt down and rubbed my thighs; they felt solid like wood, taking a pull on the cigar I thought if only I could give up the cigars and gin and tonics I would become really fit. Then after a moment I thought, hell Fred you are who you are, you have to enjoy life, everyone needs some pleasures and who wants to live until you are 80. Until, of course, you get to be 79 that is, in which case you may then have a change of heart.

After what not only seemed, but actually was, a long old day in the car, we got to Wigan to drop Bill off. After directing us through Wigan we eventually drove up his street and pulled up outside his house. As we stopped we didn't have time to open the car doors hardly before Gill had rushed out of the house, almost before we had stopped. She must have been watching through the window and it was plainly obvious she was over the moon to see him again. As we got out of the car she leapt on him, I thought she was going to crush him. We unloaded his bike and the rest of his gear and all shook hands. As I didn't work with Bill any longer this was the parting of the ways, but we were to have one more get together later, when we presented the cheque for the money raised to the Ribble Valley Ladies Luncheon Club.

John and I got back in the car and set off for Bury, we were soon on the M61 then the M60 and going through Bury to Bury Bridge where we dropped the caravan off. By then the van had done 2,200 miles since we set off and John definitely deserved a break, I must admit by this time I was feeling shattered as well. I ran him the few miles to his house and unloaded his gear, Christine was delighted to see us back and asked me in for a drink but all I wanted to do was to get home, relax and have an early night, tomorrow I would be back to work.

I waved to them as I set off, and for the first time since I had set off I actually felt alone, I switched to Classic FM on the radio and lit a cigar as I steadily cruised up the east side of the M60. As I smoked my cigar and listened to the music I felt lonely, I also felt a loss, the loss of companionship and a challenge that I had lived with for nine or 10 months.

All at once the loss of Gwen came back to me, she, of course, had been the reason I had done the ride in the first place. I think that there is never a day goes by when I don't think about Gwen, the pain doesn't get less, you just learn to deal with it, but every now and again when you are least expecting it, it strikes right at your heart and you feel the heartbreaking loss just as if it was yesterday. But then gradually, I began to think about the life I have now, I thought about Chris waiting for me at home and I realise how lucky I have been and that I have to let the pain go, otherwise all that Gwen and I had together would have been lost for the worst and not remembered for the wonderful beautiful thing it was.

Some people spend their whole lives looking for a true love and never find it, I have been lucky enough to find that elusive thing twice. As I say to Chris, I don't know what I have done in this life but it must have been something really good, because God has always been good to me.

I finally pulled up on the drive at home; I got out and opened the door, 'Is there anybody home?' I called, my standard greetings when I got home from work. Chris came out of the living room smiling and threw her arms round me.

'Welcome home love.' She said as she gave me a kiss, 'Are you glad to be home?'

'Glad to be home!' I cried, 'I can tell you now sweetheart, if I ever even so much as mention just thinking about cycling from John o' Groats to Land's End again, you can sell my bike.'

'I'll hold you to that.' She laughed as we opened both porch doors and started to unload the car.

As the days passed into weeks and the weeks into months, we got back into our old routines. The lads and women at work were glad to see me back and all wanted to hear of any excitement we may have had on our trip. They all knew the story of the locked up key as Chris had phoned them every morning after my evening phone call to her to keep them updated. Alongside the 'gooley chart' they had a large map of Britain on the wall with our route on it, so they could mark up where we were each night.

We finally got all our sponsorship money in and Bill contacted the Ribble Valley Ladies Luncheon Club to see where we could send the cheque. They were very pleased for our success, but when we suggested sending a cheque through the post they wouldn't hear of it. They informed us that they were having a fund-raising luncheon later that month and we were invited to attend as their special guests. As it didn't seem to be our scene we tried polite refusals but they weren't having any of it, 'You must all bring your good ladies too, they will really enjoy the afternoon.'

As they were so very insistent, it was agreed we would attend this fund-raising meal which was to be held at Blackburn Rovers football ground. When we offered to pay for the tickets they would not hear of it, we were told in no uncertain terms we were their guests and nothing was expected of us apart from turning up smart and the ladies, if possible, to wear hats as there was to be a competition for the best ladies' hat.

The day of the meal arrived and I must admit as we were setting off I was feeling as nervous as I did on the day we started our bike ride. After further discussions with one of the ladies from the luncheon club, Bill had told us that we would be the only three fellows there with about 120 women.

Chris and I went round the motorway to Bury to pick John and Christine up from Brandlesholme as it wasn't much out of our way going towards Blackburn. John and I were in our dinner suits and the two Christines had both got lovely cocktail type dresses and were both sporting nice big hats.

We had arranged to meet up with Bill and Gill outside the football ground in the car park as we all thought we would feel better if we went in together. We followed the signs directing us to the suite where the meal was to be held, as we went in we were greeted and ushered into the company of several of the ladies who we took to be the ones organising the meal. One of them was the lady who Bill had made contact with at the beginning and arranged to raise the sponsorship with.

After preliminary drinks, we were led to our tables and sat down awaiting the meal. As it happened we weren't the only three fellows there, the guest speaker, Andrew Collinge, was also a male. He is a very famous hair stylist and successful businessman who had developed his own range of hair products and has salons in the north west of England.

The meal was excellent and thoroughly enjoyed by all our little party, but as we were relaxing over the coffees the chairperson stood up and banged the table for quiet. She introduced her guests starting with her guest speaker and his wife and then followed by us. She gave the assembled great and good ladies a brief résumé of what we were about, what we had done and why we had done it. She then thanked us warmly for the cheque for approximately £3,500, at the end of which we got a warm round of applause. I sat there thinking how well we had done and that these 'Ladies that Lunch' must be feeling pretty pleased with our donation.

As the afternoon wore on the guest speaker got up and I must confess, though I didn't think a discussion about hairdressing would really grip my imagination, gave a performance that I found really interesting. He then provided for all the women present a bottle of his shampoo and his conditioner, finishing up with an offer for the raffle of a free hair treatment and facial at one of his salons.

Following the talk the chairperson carried out the raffle drawing the numbers for the various prizes, as usual none of them came our way but we couldn't complain having had a free meal and a very pleasant afternoon. It was decided to take the prize of the hairstyling and facial and offer it up for auction. I thought I would treat Chris and decided I would bid up to the dizzy amount of £60 but within 20 seconds, the bidding had reached £500 and though my memory fails me I seem to remember it finished up at over £1,000.

This sort of money brought tears to my eyes, over £1,000 for your hair done and a facial, Gordon Bennett! I couldn't believe my ears. Then the chairperson went on to inform the assembled ladies how much had been raised over the past few months. After feeling pretty good about our donation, within 10 minutes it felt very small change indeed. An auction at some place earlier that month had managed to raise £21,000 in an afternoon, good God! I thought, three of us slogged our guts out for eight days and Bill and I grafted for a further six months prior to the ride to raise a seventh of what they raised in an afternoon.

Despite this blow to my pride we all had a great time, everyone was really nice and treated us like royalty, so if my precious ego got a bit punctured, perhaps that was no bad thing because it brought me back to earth again and I realised what a great job these 'Ladies that Lunch' were doing and that every little helps and at the end of the day they were very grateful for our contribution.

POSTSCRIPT

Well that was the story of how I, a usually rational, sane man finished up cycling from John o' Groats to Land's End for a second time. As I said at the beginning it's not earth shattering, not even unusual but it was my story and it was something I knew I had done once and was certain I would never be daft enough to do again.

You may think, as I have many a time, stupid sod, how could he fall for something like that? Well, as I said before, don't you start to feel superior, you never know, nine months from now you may be cycling though Glen Coe and as you feel all the strength draining out of you, you may remember my words. Then you'll know how easy these things can happen and if you are cycling through I'll say this to you, good luck and God help you.

The evening after we arrived back from Land's End, I had wheeled my bike down to the garden shed, as I turned to shut the door I stopped to look at it for a moment. I thought of the miles I had ridden, the laughter and the pain, the fabulous times and the times like hell. After standing there a few minutes reminiscing, I pushed the door to and clicked the padlock shut; lighting a cigar I walked back up the garden and felt somewhat guilty as if I was shutting an old friend away. At the top of the garden I stopped and stood in the sunshine while I smoked my cigar and listened to a blackbird singing away high in the tree and a wood pigeon cooing on the fence. After a minute or two a jackdaw on the chimney top started to caw and I was instantly transported back to John o' Groats and the seagull. I was astride my bike; I could see the finger post, the hotel and little harbour as if I was there. After a moment I came round, a shiver went through me from head to toe, I pulled myself together and walked into the house. So, that was the end, as I said before, no one is ever going to get me to cycle from John o' Groats to Land's End ever again.

I met up with Bill again sometime later, when Chris and I were invited to his and Gill's wedding. It was a fabulous day and we had a really good time, and despite the occasion even on their wedding day the topic of the ride cropped up, but by this time we could both laugh about it, the memories were distant and no longer painful and I can tell you Gill had well and truly removed that chip from his shoulder.

John and Christine we still see regularly when we go caravanning, I look on John as one of my best friends. Unfortunately, he had a spell of bad health but seems to be much better now. They are still getting to Spain and watching his football team in Europe, getting about a lot and generally enjoying life to the full.

Finally, Chris and I. Well Chris is retired now and I hope she is enjoying her life with me as much as I enjoy being with her. I got made redundant almost three years ago and now work part-time seven in the morning till 11, Monday to Friday. It leaves me plenty of spare time so I've started going on my bike again, just to keep fit of course. I did manage to kick the cigar habit but fortunately still enjoy the gin and tonics; after all you have to have some pleasures in life don't you?

Generally life is as it always has been for me, brilliant, but I will own up and tell you all a secret that I have never told anyone. I have one longing that however much I try to put it out of my mind it won't go away and it's this. Whenever I start talking about cycling to anyone, I keep waiting and hoping that one day someone will say, 'Do you know Fred, I'll tell you what I've always fancied...'